Addressing Challenging Behavior in Young Children
The Leader's Role

Barbara Kaiser & Judy Sklar Rasminsky

National Association for the Education of Young Children
Washington, DC

National Association for the Education of Young Children

1401 H Street NW, Suite 600
Washington, DC 20005
202-232-8777 • 800-424-2460
NAEYC.org

NAEYC Books

**Senior Director, Publishing
& Content Development**
Susan Friedman

Director, Books
Dana Battaglia

Senior Editor
Holly Bohart

Editor
Rossella Procopio

Senior Creative Design Manager
Henrique J. Siblesz

Senior Creative Design Specialist
Charity Coleman

Senior Creative Design Specialist
Gillian Frank

**Publishing Business
Operations Manager**
Francine Markowitz

Through its publications program, the National Association for the Education of Young Children (NAEYC) provides a forum for discussion of major issues and ideas in the early childhood field, with the hope of provoking thought and promoting professional growth. The views expressed or implied in this book are not necessarily those of the Association.

Permissions

Illustration Credits

Photo Credits

Addressing Challenging Behavior in Young Children: The Leader's Role.

Library of Congress Control Number: 2020945408

ISBN: 978-1-938113-89-5

Item 1153

CONTENTS

INTRODUCTION

The stakes are high when children get kicked out of child care or elementary school: they learn that no one believes in their ability to succeed. Their learning and social and emotional development suffer, and they are put at high risk for later school failure and dropping out, even incarceration. At the same time, their families, frantic to keep their jobs and lives from crumbling, struggle to find their children new school placements or child care spots.

Research shows that suspension and expulsion disproportionately affect children of color (Office of Civil Rights 2016). As a result, some states and school districts across the country have begun to prohibit such practices with young children (Cardichon & Darling-Hammond 2019). While this enables children with challenging behavior to remain in classrooms with their peers, in many cases, their teachers may or may not have sufficient training or experience to address the behavior, recognize the effects of trauma, understand the potential impact of cultural differences, or promote social and emotional learning. Teachers depend on the support and guidance of their leaders to help them learn to teach children with challenging behavior alternative ways to express themselves.

We have been thinking about how to help leaders support their staff, children, and families in the face of challenging behavior for many years, but many factors, including political and racial unrest, climate change, and the COVID-19 pandemic, which has increased domestic violence (Evans, Lindauer, & Farrell 2020) and financial and housing uncertainty, have made this problem much more severe—and the need for solutions much more urgent, both now and in the future. In this book, we have put that need front and center. Our goal is to help administrators of programs for children from birth through 8 years old to support their staff—and the children and families they serve—in the best possible way whenever there is challenging behavior.

Leading a program for young children has never been easy, whether you're the principal of an elementary school or the director of a public or private early childhood center, preschool, or after-school or family child care program. Many early learning programs are fighting to keep afloat, and you may have neither the time nor the money to consistently do what the experts prescribe—or even have access to experts at all. Your responsibilities are endless, from too much paperwork to dealing with staff on the verge of burnout and families who naturally see everything through the lens of what's best for their own children. All of this becomes even harder when children with disruptive, even violent, behavior are in the mix.

As the head of a team, leaders play a crucial role in making it possible for children with challenging behavior to remain in school, develop positive relationships with their peers and adults, learn appropriate ways to express their needs, and be ready to learn. However, to meet these goals leaders must believe in them and have the skills to develop and lead a team that supports them. Possessing good leadership skills is just the beginning. Helping children with challenging behavior to reach their potential requires a community of caring where everyone works together and principals, administrators, directors, head teachers, supervisors, family child care providers—whatever they may be called—provide leadership and support.

Your job is to look after the educators and families while the educators and families look after the children. How do you do this? First and foremost, you need to be present—physically and emotionally. Just as working with children is all about relationships, so is working with educators; administrators need to understand themselves and their staff, the roles they each play, and the expectations of those with whom they work.

Acting as an advocate for children, staff, and families pulls you in all directions at once and requires you to understand and respect everyone's needs and challenges. Leaders must create an environment where all children and families are welcome and all staff believe that every child has the capacity to learn and behave appropriately—an environment where the educators understand both why children behave inappropriately and why they themselves respond to children's challenging behavior in the way they do.

What's in This Book?

There are plenty of books to help you as a leader organize your time, build relationships with families and staff, and deal with conflict, money, hiring, turnover, legal issues, and marketing your program. However, it is rare to find one that touches on the impact that children's challenging behavior has on other children, staff, and families as well as on the organizations involved. That is our primary focus here. Leaning on the lessons of Barbara's 40 years as a director and trainer, we concentrate on strategies drawn from research on trauma-sensitive practice, resilience, mindfulness, cultural and linguistic diversity, implicit bias, and self-reflection in addition to social and emotional learning, functional assessment, and positive behavior support.

This book offers information and strategies you can use right now, including these:

> The reasons children engage in challenging behavior

> How challenging behaviors can affect your leadership skills

> Ideas for developing a behavior guidance policy

> Ways to help staff and families understand the importance of keeping children with challenging behaviors in the program

> Suggestions for enabling your staff to act

> How to harness the power of prevention

> Methods of supporting staff through change

> Strategies for helping teachers respond effectively to challenging behavior

> Tips for working with families

> How to create a trauma-sensitive environment

In addition, we've provided a sample of a guidance policy for families and staff and several forms to document children's behavior and progress, including a behavior incident report, an observation chart for recording the antecedents of a challenging behavior as well as its consequences, and an example of a positive behavior support planning chart that can help you design effective tools to address the function or purpose of the behavior.

You may be tempted to skip to later chapters of the book for concrete advice about tackling challenging behavior, but we strongly suggest you resist. It's important to remember that the information in all of the chapters is interconnected, and there is never one single strategy or solution that works with every child, every staff member, and every family in every situation. Understanding the earlier chapters will help you to better use the ideas and strategies that come later.

Culture is a foundational part of all of our lives, and we have tried to be conscious of that fact while writing this book. Barbara has been involved with educators and administrators of different cultures over many years, including Americans of African, Latino/a, Asian, Native, Australasian, East Indian, and White European descent, in settings that were urban and rural, private and nonprofit, and run by Head Start, the military, and school districts. Still, we are aware that, as Americans of White European ancestry, we bring particular viewpoints and biases with us to this text—a fact that you, as readers, should be aware of, too. Please excuse us for using the slightly unwieldy wording "White European American" throughout the book.

How We Came to Write a Book for Leaders

Three sets of experience inspired us to undertake this task. The first is Barbara's own years leading an early childhood center that worked with children with challenging behavior. (In fact, the chapters all begin with real-life vignettes that together portray the story of a center's progress in addressing challenging behavior over many years.) The second is the experience of the many educators who have attended Barbara's workshops around the world over the past 20 years and shared their concerns about having a leader who didn't support them. The third is the experience Barbara has had with the many administrators who asked her for help when they lacked the tools necessary to provide leadership when a child with challenging behavior attended their program.

We hope our book will enable all leaders to better support and meet the needs of the educators, children, and families they serve.

Dedication

Leaders—directors of early childhood settings, family child care programs, and before- or after-school programs, and principals of elementary and primary schools—do extraordinary work every day to support the people who take care of our children. This book is for you.

CHAPTER ONE

Defining Yourself as a Leader

I (Barbara) started my teaching career inadvertently: My local school needed a substitute, and I was the only person in the rural community with a university degree.

When I asked my students in grades 7 and 8 what they hoped to be when they grew up, I discovered that they had very low expectations for themselves, and many of the girls had no professional goals at all. At the time, my daughter was almost 2 years old, and I worried that if she went through this school system, she too would have little ambition.

How could I make a difference?

I soon realized that the place to start was early childhood. With this in mind, I began the process of creating and directing what became the first government-subsidized child care program in a rural area. When we moved to the city several years later, I got a master's degree in educational administration and policy studies and founded an early childhood and after-school center for more than 120 children, which I directed for the next 20 years.

There are many routes to becoming a leader, but one thing all leaders have in common is a desire to lead. Maybe you started your career in education as a teacher and then wanted more of a voice in program decisions; or, like me, you wanted something different for your own children; or a board of directors spotted a burgeoning talent in you; or someone was needed to fill the job and you were drafted. Or maybe being the decision maker was always your goal.

Understanding Your Journey

Whatever your path to leadership, it is important for you to understand your journey. Sometimes moving from the job of teacher to being in charge of everything can be very difficult. You may have been a great teacher, but running a program calls for different skills. The transition can be especially hard if you move from teacher to administrator in the same setting. All of a sudden, your job is no longer to take care of the children but to take care of the people who take care of the children—people who used to be your coworkers but are now your staff.

When challenging behavior occurs, the people you work with—your staff, the children, and their families—need to trust you and have confidence in your skills and direction. They are counting on you to lead the way and sometimes even expect you to solve all their problems. To earn their trust, certainly you must know a lot about young children's development and learning, but you must also understand how your emotions, your past experiences, and your unconscious biases impact your decision making and daily actions. By showing that you're aware of how your feelings and life experiences affect your views and goals, you also show your staff and families that you trust and respect them. As a result, they will be more open to discussing their own priorities and goals, thereby creating a relationship built on trust. You might find that recording your actions, observations, and feelings helps to make them visible and prods you to examine them.

A ROSE BY ANY OTHER NAME

Leaders go by many names: principal, administrator, director, supervisor, head teacher, family child care provider. They do similar important work, and in this book we usually refer to them as *leaders* or *administrators*. Likewise, we use *program*, *school*, *center*, or *setting* to refer to early childhood centers, prekindergartens, elementary school programs, before- and after-school programs, and family child care programs.

Learning to Lead

Most leaders aren't born to lead—they learn to lead. Such learning requires effort, motivation, and commitment to develop basic leadership qualities such as integrity, flexibility, a positive outlook, a belief in social and racial equity, and the ability to both listen to and empower staff. An effective leader is open to feedback and isn't influenced by criticism or flattery. She is also self-reflective, intentional, visionary, and aware of her strengths and weaknesses. She looks for ways to build her own competencies and resilience; to notice and acknowledge the strengths and successes of staff, families, and children; and to help her educators reflect on their own values and perceptions.

Administrators must be able to see the broad picture and at the same time keep track of what's influencing the teachers in their program every day. All of these skills become even more important when there's a child with challenging behavior in the program.

How Do You Define Your Role?

Do you see yourself as a leader or a manager? One difference between the two is that managers have staff who work *for* them, while leaders have staff who work *with* them and contribute toward the success of the program.

Traditionally, a manager's job is to manage work—a task-based, mechanical role—while a leader's job is to influence, motivate, and enable others to contribute toward a program's success. Both roles are responsible for fulfilling the program's vision and mission, but leaders are more likely to see this work as a team effort. In the words of Antoine de Saint Exupery (1950), "If you want to build a ship, don't drum up the men to gather wood, divide the work, and give orders. Instead, teach them to yearn for the vast and endless sea."

Most effective leaders possess the skills and attitudes required both to manage and to lead. They respect the budget and complete their administrative duties, but they concentrate on innovating, inspiring, and—with their staff's input—looking for ways to solve problems and make meaningful changes when necessary.

What Is Your Vision?

The only thing worse than being blind is having sight but no vision.
—Helen Keller

Being a leader in the field of education is a very tough undertaking. For that reason—and for many others—you must care passionately about what you're doing, know why you're doing it, and know what you want your school or center to be. In short, you must have a vision.

In fact, your vision is a statement of what you want your program to be. It comes from the heart and expresses your deepest values about children, families, work, achievement, and community (Bloom 2014). It embodies your hopes and ideals and gives you a sense of purpose. At the same time, it provides an idea of what's possible and helps to guide you through difficult times. Effective leaders have a vision as well as the ability to articulate it and oversee its implementation. You are the one who can make it happen.

Your vision requires the support of your mission—that is, the approach you will use to reach your vision. Your staff, children, and families all experience your vision and your mission in the form of the values of your program and the decisions you make. An effective vision becomes all the more important when there's a child with challenging behavior in your program because, according to human resources expert Susan Heathfield (2019), a vision can inspire "enthusiasm, belief, loyalty, commitment, and excitement" by supporting staff and helping them feel that they're part of something important while also "challeng[ing] people to outdo themselves, to stretch and reach."

What Leadership Style Works Best When Challenging Behavior Occurs?

New ways of thinking about educational leadership have led to what is known variously as *facilitative, transformational, collective,* or *collaborative* leadership. Through the strength of their vision, leaders who use a version of this style inspire their staff to revise their expectations, perceptions, and motivations in order to work toward common goals. Such leaders create a partnership with their staff and grant everyone power and responsibility for supporting all children—including the child with challenging behavior.

Leading is not about having power over others but about empowering them. When there is a child with challenging behavior, it is the teachers who must work with this child, who must understand, support, and guide not only this child but also all the other children in the group. It is the facilitative leader's responsibility to provide the understanding, support, and guidance that the educators need to do their job effectively in the spirit of the program's vision.

> For years we noticed that Mondays were particularly difficult days for many of the children, especially those with behavior issues. They were excited about returning to the program and found it hard to focus. So we decided to use a staff meeting to talk about what we could do to make Mondays easier. Once we took the time to think about it together, the solution seemed simple: We didn't have to introduce new themes and activities on Monday just because Monday is the beginning of the week. Instead we scheduled more time for play, choices, and gross motor activities, and Mondays became calmer and more fun for everyone.

WORKING TOGETHER

No matter what they're called, the leadership styles mentioned in this text all basically stand for the same things. In *Five Elements of Collective Leadership for Early Childhood Professionals,* Cassandra O'Neill and Monica Brinkerhoff (2018) describe one such style, collective leadership, as a process:

> In collective leadership, there is shared responsibility and decision making, accountability, and authentic engagement. All members are involved in creating the vision and are committed to working to achieve that vision. A key aspect is that the success depends upon the leadership skills within the entire group rather than the skills of one person. (7–8)

Facilitative leadership encourages administrators to step aside so that others can step up (Sullivan 2016); to appreciate, support, and use their staff's leadership potential; and to share power and partner with educators in numerous ways. A facilitative leader gives staff a lot of say about things that affect them directly (e.g., discipline and guidance, curriculum, schedules, use of resources). Hard as it may be to avoid micromanaging, especially if you feel that you know exactly how an educator *should* respond to a child's behavior, allowing her to discover what works and what doesn't (perhaps with some gentle guidance) will enable the teacher to feel more confident and willing to try new strategies. In this way, a facilitative leader helps the staff to develop mastery, meaning, and commitment and promotes a sense of community, equity, and shared power (Bloom 2014).

"Idea architect" Jeffrey Cufaude (n.d.) offers these tips for empowering your staff:

> "Use active listening skills, including paraphrasing, summarizing, reflecting, and questioning."

> Brainstorm with your staff and help them to make connections between their own past experience and what they're learning now. Have they tried it before? What made it work?

> Honor and pay attention to everyone's unique learning style. Some staff may need one-on-one time with you, others would love articles to read, and still others may want to observe how new skills are applied.

> Handle conflicting points of view without taking sides. Recognize that what might work for one teacher may not work for another.

By using facilitative leadership, you show educators and families that you'll act in everyone's best interest when there's a problem with a child's behavior. They know that you'll be present and able to listen carefully and receptively and that you'll be prepared to support the teacher, the child, the other children, and the families. It's a tall order!

Getting to Know You

Facilitative leadership requires mutual trust and a belief in other people's abilities. There are many ways to develop these qualities, but an important one is to meet individually with each educator on a regular, informal basis to get to know him better, whether it's eating lunch together in your office during his break or catching a coffee after school—whatever works for those involved.

No doubt you have plenty of ideas for getting to know your educators and creating a partnership, but here are some questions you might ask about their work:

> What do you like most about working here?

> What are your challenges or concerns? Where do you need more support?

> "What can I do to make your job more manageable and enjoyable?" (Sykes 2016)

> "What would be the most useful thing for me to know about you as a teacher?" (Vilen 2017)

> "What do you need to feel safe, valued, and productive?" (Vilen 2017)

Because a deep, individual conversation that goes beyond short-term concerns and explores life and goals is a powerful tool, you might also try asking some personal questions: about your teachers' passions, past experiences, family lives, and their hopes and dreams—both for themselves and for the children they teach. Focus on each person's strengths and talents. Teachers feel respected when you really listen, don't interrupt, try hard to understand, and respond to them; when you give them time, tools, and support; and when you keep your promises (Carter 2016). It takes more than a single conversation to get to know each individual, so be sure to nurture those relationships.

Enhance the Climate

Leaders set the tone. One step toward building a positive climate and offering emotional support is recognizing that many of your teachers may be living with a high level of stress. Although their work is extremely important and often difficult, early childhood educators are almost unanimously underpaid, and they may be single parents and/or working a second or even third job to pay their bills, living in communities with substandard housing or high crime, and experiencing social injustices. Anything you can do to lower the stress level within the program will be useful.

Help staff to see the difference they make in children's lives; show them that you have confidence in their ability to make good choices and respect each child's gifts. Offer to let them take time off when they're having difficulty, and don't pressure them when they call in sick, even if substitutes are in short supply and you must step in to substitute yourself. You may fall a bit behind on your paperwork, but you'll have an opportunity to see what's going on in the classroom and to role-model compassion and empathy—and you'll win your staff's appreciation and loyalty. As Tomlinson (2016) advises, care for your teachers' welfare the same way they care for the children's.

Staff meetings present another opportunity to build trust, a positive climate, and a sense of teamwork. We'll discuss them in Chapter 9.

All of this will take time, but it is time well spent. The better you know your staff and the more open you are with one another, the easier it will be for you to work together to find ways to respond effectively to a child's challenging behavior.

Think About It

Book

It's unlikely that anyone possesses all the qualities in Paula Jorde Bloom's "Multi-Rater Leadership Assessment" (see For Further Learning), but this tool—which includes a long list of leadership qualities from *accessible* to *visionary*—can point to areas that need attention. Use it to evaluate your own performance and, if you're brave enough, to solicit feedback from your staff.

For Further Learning

Books

Bloom, P.J. 2014. "Multi-Rater Leadership Assessment." In *Leadership in Action: How Effective Directors Get Things Done*, P.J. Bloom, 103–7. 2nd ed. Lake Forest, IL: New Horizons.

Kouzes, J., & B. Posner. 2017. *The Leadership Challenge: How to Make Extraordinary Things Happen in Organizations*. 6th ed. San Francisco: Jossey-Bass.

MacDonald, S. 2019. *Inspiring Professional Growth: Empowering Strategies to Lead, Motivate, and Engage Early Childhood Teachers*. Lewisville, NC: Gryphon House.

Wilkinson, M. 2019. *8 Core Practices of Facilitative Leaders*. Atlanta, GA: Leadership Strategies Publishing.

Web Resource

Exchange: www.childcareexchange.com/catalog/magazine

CHAPTER TWO

What Is Challenging Behavior?

In the 1990s, when we were writing *Meeting the Challenge*, our first book on challenging behavior, we and our publisher, the Canadian Child Care Federation, applied for a grant from the Canadian justice department. Our idea was to help the government understand the connection between early intervention and later crime prevention. The department decided to fund our project, but because of its commitment to politically correct language, it wouldn't permit us to refer to young children as "aggressive." The term it accepted was "children with challenging behavior." At the time we felt like pioneers because this language was new and little used outside the field of disability. Now it extends over many pages of an internet search.

The term *challenging behavior* can mean many things. It isn't a diagnosis, and it should never be a label, because once teachers label a child as challenging (or disruptive or difficult or aggressive or uncontrollable or any other negative label), they can come to expect the child to behave in that way.

In this book, we consider as challenging any behavior that

> Interferes with a child's cognitive, social, or emotional development

> Is harmful to the child, other children, or adults

> Puts a child at high risk for later social problems or school failure
> (Klass, Guskin, & Thomas 1995; McCabe & Frede 2007)

These behaviors challenge educators because they often make it impossible to complete an activity, keep all the children safe, and provide positive reinforcement for the children who are doing their best to participate. But most teachers say a child's behavior is challenging because the strategies and interventions that work with other children don't work with this child, and they haven't been able to figure out how to change his behavior and help him get on track.

Different teachers find different behaviors challenging because everyone is sensitive to different words and behaviors, but often, when teachers' buttons are pushed, they respond in ways that escalate the problem behavior (see Chapter 5). What works for some educators probably won't work for everyone, but all of your teachers need you to listen and take their concerns seriously.

It's important for educators to understand that the behavior that challenges them is also challenging for the child. Probably more than anyone, he wants to fit in, participate in activities, and enjoy his day; but his challenging behavior is preventing him from learning the skills he needs to get along with his peers and succeed in school, and he has difficulty managing his feelings, making friends, and meeting his needs appropriately. Teachers can best deal with his challenging behavior by teaching him the skills he needs to develop self-regulation and emotional management.

Why Children Behave Inappropriately

Challenging behavior isn't as random or unpredictable as it sometimes seems. Children engage in challenging behavior for myriad reasons: they are frustrated or anxious, they don't know what else to do, the behavior is considered appropriate at home, they have language problems or a disability, or they don't know what's expected of them.

All too frequently, our instinct is to blame the family for a child's behavior. How often have you heard a teacher say, sometimes even in front of the child, "That child has no boundaries at home" or "Look at the family. What do you expect?" You can help teachers to recognize that their own implicit biases about the family may be affecting how they view the child's behavior. At the same time, it's a good idea to remind them that the family is struggling with the child's behavior every day—with probably far less training or experience than the staff. Families and early childhood educators are partners, and your job as a leader is to help your staff work with families to support their children (see Chapter 10).

Behavior Has a Function

Behavior is actually a form of communication, a child's way to meet a need or solve a problem. A child who continues to behave inappropriately does so because the behavior is working for her and meeting that need. When you and your teachers can figure out what is triggering and maintaining the behavior, you can find ways to teach the child more appropriate ways to fulfill her needs.

This is the underlying principle of functional assessment and positive behavior support, two separate strategies used together to let educators see the world through the child's eyes and decode the purpose of a challenging behavior (Chandler et al. 1999; O'Neill et al. 2015). (See Chapter 12 to learn more about these two strategies.)

Functional assessment helps you to collect data over time, which in turn enables you to identify the reason, or *function*, behind the challenging behavior. According to functional assessment, challenging behavior has three possible functions:

> **To obtain an object or attention.** When Theo knocks over Oliver's block structure, the teacher comes over to help Theo find something else to do, giving him the attention he's seeking. Theo has achieved his goal, and it doesn't matter to him whether the attention is positive or negative. Because his behavior is being reinforced, it will probably continue.

> **To avoid a person or task.** Rebecca is finding it hard to sit during circle time, and she kicks and pinches Aisha, who's beside her. The teacher reminds Rebecca to keep her hands in her lap and to herself. When she continues to bother Aisha, the teacher tells Rebecca that she'll have to leave the circle and draw or look at a book instead. Because Rebecca gets what she wants—to escape circle time—her behavior is likely to persist.

> **To change the level of stimulation.** The lights flash, the cleanup song begins, and all the children start putting things away. Everyone is moving in a different direction—it's organized chaos. Nala, who's been playing with the LEGO blocks, stands up and dumps the whole bucket of blocks on the floor. It makes a great crash, and the room quiets as everyone turns to look. The teacher tells Nala that her cleanup job is to put the LEGOs back in the bucket and return them to the shelf. The child's behavior has created the quiet she needed.

In fact, challenging behavior often occurs during transitions like cleanup or preparation for going outside, because some children find such situations overwhelming. Teachers and families often jump to the conclusion that a child's behavior is an attempt to get attention or avoid a request. They may be right, but failing to gather additional information can amplify the behavior and make it harder to teach children appropriate ways to meet their needs.

What looks like attention-seeking or avoidance may actually be the child's attempt to reduce or increase stimulation. If the environment is too noisy or chaotic, dropping a bucketful of blocks on a hard floor will instantly make the room go quiet and provide a child who's stressed an opportunity to be given a specific task to complete—putting the blocks back in the bucket. Recognizing that the child's behavior is her way of trying to control the level of stimulation will help everyone else help her to develop the skills and words to do this appropriately.

In all of these cases, if the behavior is being positively reinforced and allows the child to reach his goal and solve his problem, it will probably continue. It's crucial to remember here that the purpose behind the challenging behavior is very real to the child. He needs to have your attention or to avoid the task or to change the level of stimulation. It's important for teachers to understand that this is a given they can't change. They must respect the child's needs and teach him suitable ways to meet them. And because the purpose of the behavior can vary widely, the educator's response has to vary, too.

A Sign of Anxiety

Teachers who know a child well can probably recognize a challenging behavior on the horizon—they can see its forerunners, anxiety or frustration, beginning to emerge, although the child himself may be unaware of them. Anxiety shows itself in many ways. Some children shrink from anything that triggers fear while others may pace the room, speak very loudly or softly, or suck their thumbs. Because anxiety tends to occur during busy times of the day, it may go unnoticed and can then activate children's stress hormones, adrenaline and cortisol. These hormones prepare us to deal with imminent danger by shutting down other functions in the brain and jump-starting the fight-flight-or-freeze response—which, in children, usually manifests as a meltdown or tantrum.

Although children in this situation probably need reassurance, they often won't accept it. "The trouble is that when kids who are anxious become disruptive, they push away the very adults who they need to help them feel secure," notes Dr. Nancy Rappaport of Harvard Medical School, a specialist in mental health in school settings (Minahan & Rappaport 2012). Help teachers to understand that this is an opportunity to build a relationship and encourage them to find a way to connect with the child. This can be difficult for teachers if they take the child's behavior personally.

Spotting the anxiety early can prevent the behavior from escalating into an outburst or potentially harmful act. Something as simple as a traffic jam on the way to school or a spilled glass of milk at breakfast can be stressful for a particular child, and it is often apparent as soon as he arrives at the program that he'll have a difficult day. If you're available at arrival time, you may be able to help prevent later outbursts by supporting the teacher so that she can support the child by sitting beside him, inquiring if he'd like a hug, or asking open-ended questions. Teachers' attitudes change when they realize the child's behavior is actually the result of anxiety or fear and that he isn't trying to make things hard for them (Minahan & Rappaport 2012; Sorrels 2015).

Risk Factors for Challenging Behavior

Everyone feels anxious sometimes or might want to obtain attention or an object, avoid a task or a person, or change the level of stimulation in the environment. However, some children struggle more than others because of certain risk factors in their lives. Teachers can't change a child's life circumstances, but when they understand not only the function or purpose of challenging behavior but also why it is hard for the child to meet her needs appropriately, they can focus on responding in a way that helps her feel safe and accepted.

It's important to understand that risk factors don't cause challenging behavior, and they don't make it inevitable. Different combinations of risk factors influence children in different ways, and families and children have diverse resources and strengths that can help them through difficult situations. But risk factors do place obstacles in a child's path, and they also multiply: A child with two risk factors faces a risk for challenging behavior four times as great as a child with no risk factors (Rutter 2000).

Some risk factors may be present even before the child is born—in this book we call them biological risk factors. These include sex; temperament; pregnancy or birth complications; and neuropsychiatric problems like attention-deficit/hyperactivity disorder (ADHD), learning disabilities, autism spectrum disorder, and some genetically based emotional and behavior disorders. You may never know whether a child has one or more of these conditions, but because you've worked with many children, you're in an ideal position to notice and observe problems and advise families about the possibility of seeking a specialist's help. Having a label won't change the condition, but it will help support the family and clarify the child's behavior for the staff.

Other risk factors are environmental, having to do with family factors and parenting, poverty, exposure to violence and trauma, cultural disconnects, and the quality of education. Although we discuss them separately, biological and environmental risk factors aren't really separate entities; they constantly overlap, interact, and influence each other.

Biological Risk Factors

We start with some universal biological characteristics that are sometimes—but by no means always—risk factors. (For additional information, see For Further Learning.)

Sex

Teachers often associate challenging behavior with boys, and research tends to support this assumption. Boys seem to be more susceptible than girls to many of the risk factors for challenging behavior, including difficult temperament, ADHD, and learning disabilities (Campbell 2006; Moffitt & Caspi 2001). Some boys are already using physical force to get what they want by the age of 12 months (Baillargeon et al. 2007), and many boys engage in rough-and-tumble play, hitting, pushing, kicking, biting, teasing, and insulting each other—behavior that helps them to be accepted by their male peers (Dodge et al. 1990). This behavior—perhaps the result of the male sex hormones that bathe a boy's fetal brain—persists throughout childhood (Broidy et al. 2003). Some would argue that it is often unconsciously expected, supported, and even encouraged by adults.

It is important to bear in mind that the majority of early childhood educators are female and thus may interpret boys' behaviors as challenging when they are not. For example, when boys like each other and want to interact, they may push, yell, or call out a name to get their friend's attention. Some teachers might see this as disruptive and tell them to use an inside voice or keep their hands at their sides—interventions that may affect their sense of efficacy.

Girls usually begin to give up physically aggressive behaviors at about 2 years of age, but some continue to use physical force against their peers well into adolescence (Archer & Côté 2005), courting depression, school failure, and peer rejection (Underwood 2003). As young as age 3, girls are far more likely to turn to indirect aggression (sometimes called *relational* or *social aggression*), using covert tactics such as exclusion, back-stabbing, gossiping, and belittling to damage the self-esteem or social status of others—purposely not inviting a particular child to a birthday party, for example, or always giving her the role of the dog in dramatic play. Perhaps surprisingly, boys use these techniques almost as often as girls do (Card et al. 2008). By the time they enter kindergarten, most children have learned to regulate their feelings, control their impulses, and use their words well enough to stop using physical aggression, but 7 to 11 percent still rely on it in elementary school (Tremblay 2010).

Temperament, which is largely about the expression and intensity of emotion (Rothbart 2004), is strongly associated with challenging behavior (Frick & Morris 2004; Rothbart & Bates 2006). Temperamental traits tend to run in families, emerge early, and become relatively stable by about 3 years of age (Caspi, Roberts, & Shiner 2005). Although experience may alter them slightly, they usually endure into adulthood (Carey 2017; Caspi & Silva 1995; Tang et al. 2020).

Temperament traits don't automatically present a risk, but temperament theorist Mary Rothbart (2004) describes three dimensions of temperament that may influence the emergence of challenging behavior:

> **Negative emotionality.** Children with this temperamental trait more readily feel and express their negative emotions—sadness, anger, frustration, fear, discomfort—and are at high risk of challenging behavior. Their negative reactions can make them defiant, bring on tantrums, lead to peer rejection, and—because they often feel threatened—impair the development of their cognitive and social and emotional skills (Eisenberg et al. 2009).

> **Extraversion/surgency.** Children with this temperamental trait are inclined to be positive, cheerful, curious, active, and impulsive. They take risks and seek novelty (Rothbart 2004), and their tempers, stubbornness, and aggressive leanings make them prone to challenging behavior (Eisenberg et al. 2009). In extreme cases, they may be unable to develop empathy, guilt, or even a conscience (Frick & Morris 2004).

> **Effortful control.** This dimension includes two key abilities: the ability to focus and shift attention voluntarily and the ability to adapt to a situation by inhibiting or activating behavior. Strong effortful control may help children at risk by enabling them to manage powerful emotional and behavioral reactions—for example, they can sit still despite distractions and stop themselves from hitting a peer who grabs their racing car (Rothbart, Posner, & Kieras 2006). But a child who lacks strong effortful control may find it hard to regulate even weak feelings and impulses (Olson et al. 2005).

Because many children with extreme temperamental traits have trouble learning to manage their challenging behavior, it may be harder to teach and care for them. What matters most is how teachers respond to a child's temperament. Serious problems are more likely to arise when the expectations of the family or teacher are out of sync with the child's temperament, a concept known as *goodness of fit* (Thomas, Chess, & Birch 1968). When teachers make a point of becoming aware of their own temperaments and working to understand and accommodate a child's temperament, they can avoid letting the child's behavior get to them, choose strategies that work for her, and gradually extend her capacity to regulate her emotions and behavior, maintain relationships, and develop empathy.

Environmental Risk Factors

Although we may think of environmental risk factors as being easier to spot than biological risk factors, in fact they too can be subtle or hidden. Bear in mind that all of the other risk factors may influence what happens in the family. (See For Further Learning for more information.)

Family Factors and Parenting

Family factors can present important risks for challenging behavior and include such factors as having a very young mother; living in poverty; having parents with mental illness (especially a mother with depression), who abuse alcohol or drugs, who commit domestic violence, or who exhibit antisocial or criminal behavior; and having lost a parent through separation, divorce, abandonment, incarceration, deportation, migration, or death (Tremblay 2012). Family factors are often intensified by external events, such as exposure to violence and trauma and adverse childhood experiences (see below).

Attachment

All families love their children, but life circumstances like those mentioned above may interfere with the vital relationship between children and their families, namely children's attachment to their initial primary caregiver. According to attachment theory (Ainsworth et al. 1978; Bowlby [1969] 1982), a sensitive and responsive primary caregiver enables children to develop a secure attachment, which in turn permits them to be confident and curious, try new things, cope with challenges, and accept help and comfort when they're hurt or angry (Sorrels 2015). But when the primary caregiver is consistently unpredictable, unavailable, or rejecting, the child may form a different sort of attachment, called *insecure attachment*, and may become either demanding and clingy, with a low tolerance for frustration, or self-sufficient beyond his years and unwilling to accept help or comfort. In the most difficult circumstances (for example, when children have experienced a trauma like domestic abuse), they will form a disorganized attachment to their caregiver and may become unpredictable, hypervigilant, and highly reactive to cues in the environment (Sorrels 2015).

This being said, it's important to realize that attachment is influenced by cultural contexts and to avoid making assumptions about a child and caregiver's relationship based on the child's behavior. Teachers should also remember that children are resilient and it's possible for a teacher to become that central, consistently loving, sensitive, responsive person in a child's life. For this reason, teachers must be aware of the possible influences of attachment and focus their attention on building a relationship with the child rather than on the challenging behavior itself.

Poverty

The impact of poverty and the conditions surrounding it, which are much more prevalent among Black, Latino/a, and other families of color (Children's Defense Fund 2020), affects parenting, schools, and communities as well as individuals. In addition to the stress that these families deal with on a daily basis, their children are at greater risk to be born prematurely, with a low birth weight, and to be malnourished or exposed to lead, causing difficulty with executive functions such as memory and effortful control, and therefore with learning and regulating emotion and behavior.

Exposure to Violence and Trauma

Exposure to violence—whether firsthand, such as physical or emotional abuse, or through the media—and its strong, often traumatic effects are important risk factors for challenging behavior and have been the subject of intense interest since the release of a massive study on adverse childhood experiences (ACEs) by the Centers for Disease Control and Prevention (CDC) and health care provider Kaiser Permanente. The ACE study shows that adverse childhood experiences have a tremendous impact not only on the young children themselves but also on their health and well-being in adulthood (CDC, n.d. b; Felitti et al. 1998).

ACEs include childhood traumas such as neglect; psychological, physical, or sexual abuse; and family dysfunction stemming from a parent with substance abuse or mental illness, a mother who is a victim of domestic violence, the incarceration of a family member, and witnessing or experiencing family or community violence. Additional sources of trauma or toxic stress may include experiencing natural disasters, a pandemic like COVID-19, homelessness, discrimination, revolving foster care, bullying, repeated medical procedures, or life-threatening illness.

These experiences are frighteningly common. Almost two-thirds of the ACE study participants reported at least one ACE, and 20 percent reported three or more. Black and Latino/a children experience ACEs at a much higher rate than White European American and Asian American children do (Sacks & Murphey 2018). The more ACEs children experience in childhood, the greater their risk for social, emotional, and cognitive delays (Nicholson, Perez, & Kurtz 2019).

Structural inequities inherent in US social systems, such as education, justice, health, employment, housing, and immigration, are another important source of trauma. These inequities lead to perpetuating cycles of disadvantage and oppression and to racial and historical trauma in children of color, particularly in Black children (Sacks & Murphey 2018). (See Chapter 13 and For Further Learning.)

Although you and your teachers may never know whether a child has been exposed to trauma, a study of young children found that by 3 years of age, one in four had experienced or witnessed a potentially traumatic event, a rate that was double for children living in poverty (Briggs-Gowan et al. 2010). It is therefore wise to use a trauma-sensitive approach when working with all children.

Children who have experienced trauma may be hyperalert to threat, which can result in trouble focusing and learning, forming relationships, regulating emotions and behavior, and functioning appropriately in the classroom—all of which can make challenging behavior more likely (National Scientific Council on the Developing Child 2011). Infants may be difficult to soothe and comfort, toddlers may have temper tantrums, and preschoolers may be hypervigilant and aggressive or withdrawn (Sorrels 2015). But no matter the symptoms, behavior is a form of communication, and the best way to respond is to provide a safe and secure environment that helps the child to develop trust in you and his surroundings. (See Chapter 13.)

HIGH ALERT

The brain knows exactly what to do in a dangerous situation. It instantly activates the stress system, sending in the stress hormones cortisol and adrenaline to prepare a child to fight, flee, or freeze. As soon as the threat disappears, the stress system returns to normal (McEwen 2012).

But when a threat or traumatic event is long-lasting or intensive and there's no reliable adult around to help a child deal with it, the stress system resets itself to take over the job of defending the child at all hours of the day and night. As a result, it overloads her developing brain with toxic levels of cortisol that can disrupt the brain's architecture, impair its functioning, and even affect the child's ability to play, which is how young children learn to handle life's problems (Cole et al. 2005).

Because her stress system is always on high alert, the child sees the world as a dangerous place. Exhibiting challenging behavior is her way of protecting herself against any possible threat.

Cultural Disconnects

Culture underlies everything we see, feel, and do. Most North American schools and early childhood centers reflect the dominant culture of White Europeans, which emphasizes individualism, independence, self-direction, initiative, and competitiveness.

But different cultures have different values and norms, and children bring their cultures' skills, knowledge, and resources into the classroom. Whether intentionally or not, a program's culture, setting, policies, and practices—as well as the expectations of its educators and other staff—may ignore or fail to respect a child's culture and cultural identity. Such a gap may incline a child to feel invisible, unimportant, worthless, ashamed, or incompetent (Derman-Sparks & Edwards with Goins 2020). This disconnect and these feelings may lead some children to behave in ways that their teachers find challenging.

Today's early childhood settings are more diverse than ever, and you are probably working with families whose experiences, practices, beliefs, and values differ from your own. This may mean that you or your teachers don't fully understand the cultural values that lie behind a child's behavior or that the classroom rules or expectations do not match those of the child's home.

> Aki was a delightful 3-year-old. At nap time, however, there was literally no way to get him to lie down on his cot for more than a minute. All the other children would be ready to rest, some with a book and others already nodding off, when Aki would get up, run around the room, tickle his friends, and laugh.
>
> When I spoke with his mother, she smiled and said that Aki had never slept in a bed of his own. In the Japanese culture, children sleep with their parents in the family bed.
>
> From then on, a teacher always lay on the floor beside Aki's cot at nap time, and he happily drifted off to sleep.

When you and your staff do not speak a family's language, the door for misunderstanding may open wider. Such a situation may make it hard to discuss the child's behavior with the family. If implicit bias leads you or your staff to assume that poor parenting—rather than cultural factors—caused the child's behavior, a wall may grow between you and the family.

Honest discussions with your teachers are probably the best way to start breaking down this barrier. Make the implicit as explicit as possible. Help them to understand the cultural values of the child's family as well as their own and how those values affect everyone's feelings and reactions to the child's behavior. For example, when educators set goals for the children without consulting the family, the goals may not reflect what the family is hoping their child will learn from their experience in the program. It's important to remind teachers to include families in the goal-setting process. (See Chapter 5, where we discuss culture in more detail.)

In addition, you can aid teachers' efforts to

> Cultivate caring relationships with children

> Develop culturally responsive teaching strategies that recognize and support children's cultures and experiences

> Set high standards and expectations for everyone

Poor-Quality Early Childhood Programs

In 2020, COVID-19 changed our world, starkly revealing systemic social and racial inequities in the United States, including those in early childhood education. Low-quality early childhood programs and schools—struggling with inadequately trained staff, large class sizes, inappropriate teaching strategies and behavioral expectations, a lack of access to the help of a mental health professional as well as basic materials—also pose a risk for children's behavior.

As a leader and a caring adult, you are an important role model. Your staff will watch how you respond to the child with challenging behavior and to her family. With your support and example, your teachers will come to realize that challenging behavior is the result of factors in children's and families' lives that they can't control. This understanding may increase teachers' empathy, enhance the quality of their relationships with both children and families, and enable them to help the children learn the skills they need to blossom into the fully functioning people they all deserve to become.

For Further Learning

Derman-Sparks, L., & J.O. Edwards. With C. Goins. 2020. *Anti-Bias Education for Young Children and Ourselves*. 2nd ed. Washington, DC: NAEYC.

Gonzalez-Mena, J. 2008. *Diversity in Early Care and Education: Honoring Differences*. 5th ed. Washington, DC, & New York: NAEYC & McGraw Hill.

Harris, N.B. 2019. *The Deepest Well: Healing the Long-Term Effects of Childhood Adversity*. Boston: Mariner Books.

Kaiser, B., & J.S. Rasminsky. 2017. *Challenging Behavior in Young Children: Understanding, Preventing, and Responding Effectively*. 4th ed. Columbus, OH: Pearson Education.

Lynch, E.W., & M.J. Hanson, eds. 2011. *Developing Cross-Cultural Competence: A Guide for Working with Children and Their Families*. 4th ed. Baltimore: Brookes.

Powell, B., G. Cooper, & K. Hoffman. 2016. *The Circle of Security Intervention: Enhancing Attachment in Early Parent-Child Relationships*. New York: Guilford Press.

Sorrels, B. 2015. *Reaching and Teaching Children Exposed to Trauma*. Lewisville, NC: Gryphon House.

York, S. 2016. *Roots and Wings: Affirming Culture and Preventing Bias in Early Childhood*. 3rd ed. St. Paul, MN: Redleaf Press.

CHAPTER THREE

How a Child with Challenging Behavior Impacts Your Leadership Skills

As the center's director, I'd always had full responsibility for keeping everyone safe, finding new ways to support the teachers, and reassuring families that we were providing a safe, caring, and stimulating environment for all the children. But after Andrew arrived at the center at age 2½—and for the following three years—I took a deep breath at the end of each day, thankful that all the children were going home in one piece.

We lived from crisis to crisis. Andrew hit and pushed other children and destroyed their block structures. He didn't respond to our usual interventions. Angry parents threatened to withdraw their children, and several frustrated staff members wanted to expel Andrew or considered changing careers. Others worried that he occupied so much of their time that they had none left to spend with the children who were behaving appropriately, and they felt that his presence kept them from achieving outcomes they desired for the other children.

I had to take a hard look at my priorities. I knew I had to listen closely to all the teachers and respect their thoughts and feelings while we figured out what to do. I didn't agree that the solution was to ask Andrew to leave. Where would he go? How would this make him feel? Would I just be adding stress to the family? So I began my search for the perfect solution: either a totally new one, or the solutions that other centers and schools had already found. We had to get back to our roots and revisit the center's philosophy, vision, and mission as well as the policies that guided us. All of us had to take ownership of the problems brought out or created by a child with challenging behavior. This was bound to take time—there were no shortcuts.

Finding Ways to Welcome a Child
with Challenging Behavior

Regardless of your official title, one of the most important aspects of leadership is the responsibility you hold for the welfare of everyone in the program. Usually this isn't an onerous task, but it can become overwhelming when a child is hurting others or constantly disrupting activities. The educators need to feel supported and understood; the other children need to feel secure; their families need to believe that their children are safe and happy; and the family of a child with challenging behavior needs to believe that no one is judging them and be willing to work with you and the teachers. This situation calls for your very best leadership skills and your total commitment. You now have to become an even better and more intentional leader.

Start with yourself. Do you think a child with challenging behavior should remain in your program? The answer is important, because your attitude affects how your staff think about whether or not the child should stay. If you allow him to stay, you may find yourself standing alone, and you may be second-guessing yourself whenever there's a disturbing incident with the child or a family complains about him. On the other hand, you'll be fulfilling a moral and ethical obligation to help the child, following the underlying principles of NAEYC's Code of Ethical Conduct, acting as a positive role model for your staff, and showing the teachers you believe in their ability to overcome difficulties and uncover the child's potential.

This is not an easy decision to make, especially without staff or board support. Such a huge commitment will likely change everyone's priorities. Even if your state or school district requires you to keep the child in the program and you feel strongly that you want him to stay because you believe it's the right thing to do, it's important to get your teachers on board. Give them some time to think about what this decision will mean for the child and the family, now and in the future. What messages will it send to the staff? To the families? To the children? Together with your teachers, consider the pros and cons of the situation—with the proviso that you'll develop a long list of pros and won't let the discussion deteriorate into a gripe session. That is, you'll guide the teachers so that they see the benefits of keeping the child at the school or center.

Find out what your teachers need to know in order to believe that they can really help this child and continue to keep everyone safe. What additional information do they need about him? What role do they want you to play? Are you willing and can the center afford to hire additional staff or a specialist? Your leadership skills and your relationship with your teachers and families will be especially important if you live in a state or school district where it is not permissible to suspend or expel a young child from an early childhood program. How will you and your teachers come to terms with this reality? Do you believe that they can learn the skills they need and that you can work together with the family?

You may choose to bring in a teacher assistant, shadow teacher or aide, resource teacher, or speech and language therapist who would work directly with the child or to arrange for a mental health consultant or coach to work with staff. It's wise to consider these options *before* your staff becomes burned out and feels frustrated and helpless—a state of affairs that may prevent them from hearing anything the expert suggests. Instead, ask them and the family how they feel about this idea (and obtain the family's consent), and in the meantime find out what support your state or school district provides and if there are other agencies you can contact. Although the mental health professionals in this field are well trained and do excellent work, be aware that they may serve a very large territory and carry an enormous caseload, sometimes making their visits farther apart than you'd like. It's wise to prepare in advance for the bureaucratic and monetary hoops such a move may require you to jump through. (See Chapter 9 for more information.)

A LONG LIST OF PROS

If your educators need further convincing beyond the argument that it's the moral and ethical thing to do to keep a particular child in the program, remind them of the differences they can make in this child's life by helping her to

> Develop stable, supportive relationships with adults who care for and teach her

> Spend time in the presence of children who act as positive role models and teach her social and emotional skills and how to make friends

> Practice the skills she needs for learning and later schooling, such as listening and following instructions, managing her feelings and her behavior, and asking for help (Zinsser 2018)

> Find and utilize her strengths (because every child has them)

> Avoid having to endure a massive rejection that she doesn't understand and that causes her and her family to think of her as bad or unworthy (Jones & Levin 2016)

> Get on a path to academic and personal success in the future

> Obtain access to special services such as mental health consultation, early intervention, or special education, if needed

In short, they will be helping the child enjoy a vital learning experience (Jones & Levin 2016).

Point out that the teachers will experience benefits as well. They will

> Recognize that they already have the skills—or will acquire new ones—that will help them become better teachers

> Learn skills that will lower their stress level and enable them to teach with more confidence

> Have the satisfaction of knowing that they've given the child (and even the family) a better chance at a successful and productive life

> Help the other children develop the social and emotional skills—and the flexibility—to interact with a variety of peers

---

Being in the Classroom

If you're committed to going forward with keeping a child in the program, how will you provide your teachers with the support, information, and training they need to work with her effectively?

The only way to really know and understand the child and the issues the teachers are dealing with is to spend time in the classroom yourself. Despite the endless administrative duties facing you, it's imperative to find this time—and to go so often that the educators don't see your presence as a token gesture. They spend every day working with this child who hits classmates or continually disrupts activities, while you can come and go as you please. Although you're no doubt giving the teachers helpful feedback, this situation can breed resentment, and you may unintentionally be alienating the very people you're trying to support.

The solution is to become an integral part of the classroom, entering every classroom every day so that both children and teachers feel at ease having you around and don't alter their behavior in your presence. If you appear only after challenging behavior arises, you'll miss vital clues about its origin. Of course, you should also make sure to be there during the times your teachers have identified as difficult, such as transitions, story time, or nap time.

Create both special and routine opportunities to be with each group. Assign yourself a specific task or ask your teachers what you can do to be useful and part of the scenery, such as working with a group of children, organizing shelves, joining in at story or circle, making snack, or helping out during transitions. Spend enough time at it so that you become invisible.

Because you're already overburdened with tasks, it makes sense to schedule this time on your calendar so that it becomes part of your day rather than an added responsibility. To avoid conflicts, arrange your other responsibilities around it. If possible, try to sub whenever a teacher is absent.

Another thing you can do is provide formative and informal feedback to teachers after your classroom visits. When you do this regularly, it is less threatening and easier for them to accept. You don't need to find something to say after each visit, but if you see something that deserves suggestions or positive feedback, such as how a teacher responded when one child kicked another, be sure to find a few minutes out of the children's hearing—in the hall, during nap time, or later in the day—to discuss the incident, especially if the teacher handled it well. The harder the teachers are struggling to respond effectively to problem behavior, the more important it is for you to make these classroom sojourns (Carter 2016; Sykes 2016).

When Differences Arise

To prevent or respond to a child's challenging behavior, you and you staff should develop a common approach that they help to shape and can support. Even if you've worked together smoothly for years, a child with challenging behavior can shake up everyone and everything. Working with children with challenging behavior pushes educators' buttons, and this is when differences surface—differences in culture, race, class, religious beliefs, and political views; in the ways people were raised and educated; in experience, temperament, and support; and, of course, in values and education philosophy.

TIME WELL SPENT

In "The Why and When of Walkthroughs," third grade teacher Paul Murphy (Murphy & George 2018) tells his principal that she doesn't visit their classrooms frequently enough. This means she has no context for understanding what's happening there, which in turn leads her to make wrong assumptions. He begs her to ask him why she's seeing what she's seeing in his classroom:

> "You don't know what happened five minutes, five hours, five days, five weeks, or five months before you walked in.

> "So ask me why. Ask me why because you don't know. . . . Because if you don't ask, many of your teachers won't tell you. They don't want to rock the boat. They don't want to come off as whiners. . . .

> "By making a habit of asking why and truly listening, you honor the individuality of our students and complexity of our craft as teachers." (2–3)

Are you spending enough time in the classroom to see what's really going on there? Would your teachers feel comfortable talking to you in such a candid way? What do you think they would say? If you suspect they'd be reluctant to speak up, what can you do to change things?

Teachers' different behavioral expectations and responses to children's behavior can become major factors in the way that children behave. And when the behavioral requirements of the classroom are quite different from those at home, in the everyday world, and even in before- and after-school programs, the feedback that children receive about their behavior is often inconsistent and confusing and may actually provoke inappropriate behavior as they test their limits. These differences may also lead to teachers seeing their decisions undermined by colleagues or supervisors.

Rather than attempting to change people, you and your staff together must evaluate how best to respond to each child. What's important is that everyone—educators, administrators, cooks, bus drivers, office staff—be able to identify the children's behaviors that annoy or provoke them and to control their own responses so that everyone can work together toward the team's goals. It's especially important for you as the leader to remember that each person's response to a child's behavior is valid and should be not only recognized but also understood and respected.

Building a Team

So, what can you do to create a strong, unified team that treats each child, including the one with challenging behavior, as a valued individual? Listening is crucial. The members of your team need to believe you're there to support them and that you'll acknowledge and respect their personal and professional knowledge and their unique contributions. That means you'll have to know them well.

BACKING YOUR STAFF

How can you help your staff in their quest for personal and professional development? Bearing in mind that each staff member has a different personality, experience, and culture, attend to the following:

> Be a good listener.

> Respect each person's perspective.

> Help staff to respect one another.

> Be aware of what interests each person.

> Use everyone's talents and strengths.

> Empower and encourage staff to take initiative and be creative.

Developmental Stages of Teaching

There is little doubt that most teachers looking back at their first year of teaching can see that they have improved at their jobs. We learn by doing. Many years ago, Lilian Katz (1972) created a framework for what she called "developmental stages of teachers" (see the figure on the next page) that remains a helpful guide to working with both individual educators and the team as a whole. Paula Jorde Bloom and colleagues (Bloom, Hentschel, & Bella 2013) argue that new teachers do better with directive supervision, whereby you provide the structure and information teachers need to ramp up their confidence and skill. As teachers gain experience, your involvement can become more collaborative and a partnership can develop. In contrast, seasoned teachers know what they need to do to improve their own practice and how they can help their less experienced colleagues.

DEVELOPMENTAL STAGES OF TEACHERS		
Developmental Stage	**Professional Stage**	**Supervisor Role**
Survival—teachers who are struggling to get through the day and be accepted by their colleagues	New teachers	Provide directive supervision.
Consolidation—teachers with growing skills and confidence who are able to address children's problems	Teachers with a few years of experience	Enable and encourage collaboration with their colleagues.
Renewal—teachers ready to profit from educational opportunities and new techniques	Teachers on the brink of burnout, unchallenged, and perhaps considering a career change	Help find more challenging responsibilities and new opportunities for growth.
Maturity—teachers who encourage and inspire others and are still finding new insights	Teachers ready to take on more responsibility for others	Set up a mentoring program together.

Adapted from Katz 1972, 50–53

If you offer your teachers appropriate ideas and opportunities, you can leverage these diverse levels of expertise to pull your team together. For example, you might encourage an educator with many years of teaching under his belt to pair up with a less experienced teacher who is still struggling to meet the needs of the children in her group and may not yet have acquired the skills to cope with a child's challenging behavior. You may make an experienced teacher on the brink of burnout feel more valued if you ask her to propose possible changes to the program and physical environment that could help to prevent challenging behavior. She will likely come up with inspired and constructive ideas—and as her colleagues carry out her suggestions, the team will coalesce around her.

Degrees of Teacher Control

Another basic difference may arise in your educators' views about teacher control (see "Mission Control," page 26). Every teacher has distinct behavioral expectations based on his individual experiences and culture and will teach and respond to children according to his own values and beliefs. It is important for all the teachers—and for you—to understand where each of them fits on the continuum from low- to medium- to high-control methods or punishment. For example, a medium-control teacher is likely to believe in consequences for disruptive behavior and think that the consequences should be directly related to what the child has done (such as getting ice to help care for a child he has hit). But a teacher who advocates high-control methods may want to apply consequences that aren't necessarily related to the behavior, such as limiting recess or sending the child to the office.

MISSION CONTROL

Different educators believe in different degrees of teacher control when it comes to addressing behavior. These are known as low-, medium-, and high-control methods.

> *Low-control* methods, usually called *guidance*, are based on attachment theory, constructivism, and the psychology of Carl Rogers; they are typified by the work of Haim Ginott, Thomas Gordon, Alfie Kohn, and Marilyn Watson. Adherents believe children can construct their own values and knowledge and make their own choices and that misbehavior occurs when children's needs aren't being met or when they lack the skills to solve their problems. Teachers facilitate development by attending to children's feelings, thoughts, and ideas (Greene 2010; Watson with Ecken 2003).

> *Medium-control* methods by teachers are often referred to as *discipline*. Rooted in the theory of Alfred Adler and reflected in the perspectives of Rudolf Dreikurs, William Glasser, Richard Curwin, and Allen Mendler, these methods rely on the idea that both internal and external forces govern children's development and that children misbehave because they have mistaken ideas about how to belong to the group. In this view, children learn to behave appropriately by understanding the consequences of their decisions (Burden 2017).

> *High-control* methods, also known as *behavior management*, come from the behavior modification theory of B.F. Skinner and the social learning theory of Albert Bandura and include methods advocated by Lee and Marlene Canter. Followers believe that children learn by observing and imitating the people around them and that it is the teacher's responsibility to help them control their behavior by making and enforcing rules, reinforcing appropriate behavior, and applying consequences for inappropriate behavior (Burden 2017).

It's important to note that punishment is never appropriate and is not what we mean by more control. As NAEYC's Code of Ethical Conduct states, "Above all, we shall not harm children. We shall not participate in practices that are emotionally damaging, physically harmful, disrespectful, degrading, dangerous, exploitative, or intimidating to children. *This principle has precedence over all others in this Code*" (NAEYC 2016, 8).

Some children may function better with less control; others need more. It is natural for teachers to believe that their own way is best. But depending on the child and her relationship with the educator, too much or too little control can trigger challenging behavior, and a teacher's natural style may support or hinder that child's ability to function. As Bloom, Hentschel, and Bella (2016) point out, "Our perceptions become our reality" (36), and it's hard to see things in a different way.

It is vital for you to understand where your educators are coming from and to know what kind of support each of them needs. Although there is never just one way to respond to a behavior, some responses are more effective than others. Some educators may be waiting for your guidance, and others may resist trying something different, even when they know that what they're doing doesn't work. This is when your presence in the classroom, your ability to role-model appropriate responses, and your relationship with the teacher are essential to helping her to find a better way to respond. It's important for everyone to remember that there's more than one way to do things.

Developing a Common Approach to Challenging Behavior

Ultimately, early childhood programs are all about relationships. Families must be able to place their trust in everyone—in you as the leader and in all the teachers and support staff. Because providing the best possible care and learning environment takes teamwork, it is imperative for staff to trust you and each other—to know they can be open with and rely on one another,

especially when there's a child with challenging behavior in the classroom. If you've already lived through this experience, you understand just how important it is for staff to work together, share ideas, and support one another.

Relationships built on trust, mutual respect, empathy, and a belief in the other person's ability are the keys both to facilitative leadership and to building a common team approach. And once again, as the leader you set the tone.

Your relationships with your teachers act as a model for the relationships teachers can develop with the children and their families. Each teacher needs to know that you care about him as a person—each one's story is unique, and you need to hear them all. This is always important to good leadership, but it's especially important when there's a child with challenging behavior in the program because these positive relationships can prevent the child's presence from creating rifts and cliques among the staff.

Working Together

It's also essential to have conversations with the team as a whole. One of the best ways to build trust with your teachers is to show that you trust them first (Berkowicz & Myers 2017b). Create a safe and comfortable space for them to store their belongings, prepare their lessons, or just sit and relax, and construct frequent chances for them to meet and talk as a group. Make it clear that you don't have all the answers, that it's important for them to express their thoughts and feelings—and that you won't be judging them. It should also be easy for them to ask for advice and to share information, resources, and ideas about pedagogy (Bloom, Hentschel, & Bella 2016). Identify and work with their concerns and provide them with ways to be successful and meet their goals.

Just as it's important for you to know your staff, it's also important for them to know their colleagues' life stories. Hearing about one another's struggles and joys helps staff to bond, find common ground, and figure out how they can learn and work together even when they disagree. It is often less threatening to open up in a group of peers than in a one-on-one session with the director. Some people are willing to share and even enjoy sharing and connecting the dots; others are more private and require a higher level of trust before they'll confide in either you or the group; still others are never comfortable sharing personal information. Remind staff that most people who work with young children are nurturers and will probably understand their challenges and support them through their journey. Margie Carter and Deb Curtis (2010) suggest reading children's books and sharing memories of childhood experiences as a way to jump-start these conversations. Be aware of and sensitive to the reality that individuals' childhoods may have involved trauma that remains unaddressed.

You might find that not all the teachers have the same experience with a particular child. What makes the difference? Why do some teachers find certain children's behavior challenging and others either find effective ways to respond to it or do not see the behavior at all? Encourage the teachers to investigate their colleagues' strategies and put them to use throughout the program. Talk with them about children's behaviors that push their buttons and help them think about the connection between a particular button and the way their own families viewed a particular behavior (Aguilar 2017).

Bringing these varied perspectives together in a way that supports the philosophy of the program can be a daunting task, but once staff know and trust you—and know that you trust them—you can promote discussion that helps them figure out how they can work together. Good teaching thrives in a collaborative learning environment, so create opportunities at staff meetings, breaks, and planning time for them to discuss individual children, give each other feedback, work together on projects, talk about core values, revisit goals—and change plans if necessary.

Reconciling Differences

Bloom and colleagues suggest that when disagreements occur, it's best to encourage "a frank, open discussion about different points of view. Help the parties understand that one person doesn't have to be wrong for the other one to be right—that we all have a piece of the truth and that truth is usually shaped by the way we interpret the information we have" (Bloom, Hentschel, & Bella 2016, 42).

Especially if your teachers have opposing values, finding common ground is neither quick nor easy. Core values—each person's deeply held views of what's important and worthwhile—act as a moral compass for decision making and reflect the person's unique life, summing up her particular family, culture, experience, education, and society (Bloom 2014). It will probably require many months of talk for each individual to discover and clarify her own core values for herself.

A good place to start is with Bloom's "Beliefs and Values Questionnaire" (2014; see For Further Learning), which helps teachers think about their attitudes toward children, families, and their own teaching by considering open-ended questions such as "I think children are generally . . ." or "The most important thing a teacher can do is . . ."

Not only will this process enable you to understand why people behave the way they do, it will also allow you to arrive at a place where you can agree about what you all value and want to work toward—that is, to work together to develop a set of shared values for your program (Bloom 2004).

Sadly, turnover is inevitable in the early childhood field, and at some point you will no doubt have to add a new teacher to your staff. When there is a child with challenging behavior in the program, it becomes increasingly necessary for everyone to work together, and hiring the right people is a crucial part of creating a cohesive team. It is important for new teachers to understand and share your core values. Their belief systems should align with yours, but they shouldn't be clones either. Diverse backgrounds, experiences, skills, and points of view stimulate insight and growth and lead to innovative problem solving, so it is essential to balance these qualities as you make your choice (Harvard Business School 2017).

It is clearly a formidable task to keep everything together while getting your staff on board and even integrating a new teacher, but if you've created a sense of teamwork focused on a common goal that's based on an understanding of what you expect from your staff and what they expect from you, it is possible to work together and support the children, their families, and your teachers.

For Further Learning

Bloom, P.J. 2014. "Beliefs and Values Questionnaire." In *Leadership in Action: How Effective Directors Get Things Done*, P.J. Bloom, 101–2. 2nd ed. Lake Forest, IL: New Horizons.

Feeney, S., & N.K. Freeman. 2018. *Ethics and the Early Childhood Educator: Using the NAEYC Code*. 3rd ed. Washington, DC: NAEYC.

Feeney, S., N.K. Freeman, & E. Moravcik. 2016. *Teaching the NAEYC Ethical Code: A Resource Guide*. Rev. ed. Washington, DC: NAEYC.

Gordon, J. 2018. *The Power of a Positive Team: Proven Principles and Practices that Make Great Teams Great*. Hoboken, NJ: Wiley.

CHAPTER FOUR

Developing a Behavior Guidance Policy

> As required by state licensing, our program had a policy and procedures handbook that explained our vision, mission, and other daily requirements, including a guidance policy that we'd created before a child with challenging behavior attended the center. After our experience with Andrew, we realized that we needed to revise and expand the policy. The best way to undertake this job was with input from the staff and families on the board of directors.

Children deserve early childhood settings that are safe, supportive, and conducive to teaching and learning. Most states and NAEYC Early Learning Program Accreditation standards require early childhood programs to develop policies and procedures that provide a framework for their overall operation and create guidelines for dealing with whatever issues and concerns may arise, from negotiating staff salaries to changing diapers to ensuring children's social and emotional learning.

Although policies and procedures are especially important when it comes to guiding children's behavior, a recent survey of 2,000 educators showed that "most districts and schools do not have a clearly communicated and consistently followed protocol for managing behavioral disruptions," or if they do have one, the guidelines often don't reach school administrators or teachers, leaving them feeling unprepared and unsupported (District Leadership Forum 2019, 3).

In addition, the federal government and various states have developed guidelines to bring discipline equity to young children of color, and many of these guidelines eliminate suspension and expulsion (HHS & ED 2016). The issues behind these guidelines present a compelling argument for re-examining your policy and how it's applied.

Although the heart of guidance lies in relationships, it is essential to develop and constantly update a policy that clarifies how an early childhood program will prevent and address challenging behavior. As the leader, you are responsible for ensuring that your center or school has such a policy and that everyone understands and adheres to what's in it.

An effective behavior guidance policy sets out guiding principles and expectations that support the social, emotional, and academic success of all children (Longstreth & Garrity 2018). At the same time, it announces your priorities to stakeholders—staff, families, sponsoring organizations,

and the community—and serves as a vital tool for teachers, helping them to prevent, address, and correct behavior by outlining rules and strategies as well as acceptable and unacceptable conduct for children and adults alike. Appendix 1 contains an example of a guidance policy.

With a clear policy that everyone commits to following, guidance is less subjective and confusing for both staff and families. No one feels picked on and no one thinks you're making up the rules as you go along (for example, when you refuse a parent's—or a teacher's—demand that you expel a child with challenging behavior).

Start with Your Vision and Mission

As you saw in Chapter 3, educators have different views about how to address children's behavior. Your guidance policy should reflect the philosophy of your program—a philosophy you've probably already thought a lot about and refined in your vision and mission statements, which form the basis for leadership decisions and should also be the basis for your guidance policy.

Whether you're writing a brand-new policy or revising an old one, this task presents an excellent opportunity for administrators, staff, and families to get together and talk about their beliefs, values, assumptions, and biases and to establish a shared foundation for daily life at the school or center. This collaboration makes everyone's acceptance of the finished policy more likely, and once you've written a draft, you can increase buy-in by offering other staff, families, board members, and alumni the chance to review it (and be sure to take their feedback into consideration!) (LeeKeenan & Ponte 2018).

Focus on Prevention

The surest way to address challenging behavior is to prevent it from occurring in the first place, so your policy should focus first on prevention and point to qualities that promote prosocial behavior: a positive social climate; caring, responsive teacher–child relationships; a comfortable, welcoming physical environment; engaging activities and materials; and predictable schedules and routines.

Social Climate and Relationships

Because children rely heavily on the external environment for clues about how to behave, a positive school climate and a culture of community where everyone belongs and supports one another foster both learning and positive behavior. Your policy should describe the importance of climate and relationships along with examples of how to create them. For instance, Terada (2018) suggests that teachers "greet each child by name with a smile and a welcoming comment at the classroom door" and "make transitions fun and part of the learning experience."

Your policy can actively promote appropriate behavior and self-regulation by stating that a goal of your program is to teach positive behavior and social and emotional skills and to give children plenty of chances to practice them, both in regular classroom exchanges and through the use of a social and emotional learning program. Teachers should role-model positive behavior and self-regulation and employ these evidence-based strategies:

> Reinforcing positive behavior with words and gestures

> Having clear, predictable expectations that are culturally, linguistically, and ability appropriate for each child

> Using active listening and redirection

> Helping children use conflict resolution strategies

> Providing children with choices, reminders, and a place to go if they feel they need some time away from the group

Every program should also have three to five clear, short rules that are worded positively and let the children know what *to* do. (See page 52.)

In addition, policies should highlight culturally responsive teaching, which supports the diverse abilities children bring from home and enables them to feel accepted, valued, and competent. Because cultural expectations influence both teachers' and children's definitions of appropriate behavior, the policy should stress the following strategies:

> Teacher self-reflection and recognition of cultural bias (Gregory, Skiba, & Mediratta 2017; NAEYC 2019; Weinstein, Tomlinson-Clarke, & Curran 2004)

> Working with families and learning about their cultures and languages

> Using curricula, instruction, and assessment that meet diverse learning needs (e.g., partner and small group learning rather than whole group activities)

> Classroom management that synchronizes with children's culture—for example, telling students what to do rather than asking them to do it (e.g., "Please sit down" versus "Can you please sit down?"; tossing out the question mark makes all the difference, clearly indicating that this is a command, not a choice).

Environment and Program

It's also important to identify environmental features that support social development and positive behavior, such as a physical layout with learning centers and clear pathways, consistent routines, predictable schedules, engaging curriculum, and materials that reflect the variety of children's abilities and cultures.

Intervention Strategies

When you're discussing both prevention and intervention, your guidance policy should emphasize that challenging behavior is a child's way to communicate and her solution to a problem (see Chapter 2). Once again, this policy should present well-defined, appropriate, and consistent expectations and consequences and identify as clearly as possible how everyone will respond to behavior in ways that are fair, equitable, and aimed at teaching children new skills that enable them to fulfill their needs in an acceptable fashion.

To avoid creating guilt, shame, or low self-esteem in a child, teachers' corrections should instruct the child and focus on the behavior, not the child herself. But before setting limits, educators should acknowledge the child's feelings—for example, "You look angry. But I can't let you hurt Charlotte" (British Columbia Day Care Action Coalition & Early Childhood Educators of British Columbia 2016). In addition, the policy should specifically outlaw the use of humiliation and punishment, which can lead to guilt, shame, or low self-esteem and does not teach prosocial behavior or reduce challenging behavior.

Many schools and early childhood centers across the country have adopted a school- or program-wide tiered intervention approach, such as Positive Behavioral Interventions and Supports (PBIS) or the Pyramid Model for Supporting Social Emotional Competence in Infants and Young Children. To deliver these interventions, staff must be trained and understand how to collect behavioral data.

In addition to reducing challenging behavior, PBIS and the Pyramid Model reduce suspension and expulsion, but when used on their own, they fail to erase the disproportionate use of these consequences with children of color. It is therefore important to augment them with the culturally responsive strategies identified earlier (Gregory, Skiba, & Mediratta 2017; Skiba & Losen 2015–2016). (We discuss culturally responsive strategies throughout the book, but see especially Chapter 5.)

Before identifying the strategies the program will implement, discuss with your staff why some strategies have worked in the past and others have not. (See Chapters 11 and 12 for more about intervention strategies.)

HANDLE WITH CARE

One center's guidance policy includes this warning:

"Each step taken in the behavior guidance process must also be implemented over a reasonable period of time. The process cannot be sped up to attain a desired expectation. Changes in behavior often take time and every effort should be made to have the patience required to effect the desired change" (Quesenberry, Hemmeter, & Ostrosky 2011, 216).

The Role of Families

Families are children's first and most important teachers, and their role in their children's lives must be recognized and respected. Your guidance policy should describe how the program will communicate with families and establish proactive, collaborative relationships before challenging behavior appears. It should also define the steps the staff and administration will take to address challenging behavior, such as delineating how, when, and by whom the family will be contacted for meetings and explaining the data that needs to be collected about the behavior—its frequency, intensity, and response to interventions—so that you and your teachers can discuss the problem accurately. This is especially critical when you'd like to obtain permission to bring in an outside consultant to observe a child. In this case, you and the teacher should meet with the family and help them to see that another, objective, professional perspective will help the teacher to find more ways to support their child.

In the policy, state that all information about children and families is confidential. If family members are concerned about the impact of another child's behavior on their own child, remind them of the rule of confidentiality and tell them about the measures you've put into place to ensure the safety of all the children.

It is important for families to know what's in the guidance policy and have the opportunity to discuss any concerns they may have, so upon registration give them a copy to read and take home. To confirm that they have read it, both you and they should sign this copy and one additional copy, which will remain in the child's file. This precaution can avoid confusion and anger when there is a child with aggressive behavior in the program.

Supporting Staff

The guidance policy should commit the program to supporting the staff through ongoing training and professional development that allows them to implement the policy and improve their practice. It should pay particular attention to helping teachers become aware of their implicit bias and treating all children fairly and equitably (Longstreth & Garrity 2018). Because teachers who are stressed are more likely to use inappropriate disciplinary tactics, the policy should also prioritize the staff's own health and well-being (Gilliam & Shahar 2006).

School and center leaders are responsible for ensuring that staff members read and agree to implement the guidance policy before they start work. Review it with staff annually and go over proposed changes together. Remember that a written policy is a guide, not a contract— some teachers will follow it and others may not. It's therefore wise to monitor each educator through regular observation, supervision, or staff meetings.

Mental Health Consultation

Although many early childhood programs currently have no access to a mental health consultant, it is in everyone's best interest to try to acquire this service. For this reason, your policy should provide guidelines for using a consultant in the event that the possibility arises. In order for the consultation to be effective, it's vital to have both the explicit support of the teachers and the permission of the family, which are critical for enabling everyone to utilize the expert's advice.

Collecting Data

Collecting data on behavior incidents can help programs deal with individual children and at the same time become a tool for avoiding biased judgments and for making different teachers' guidance decisions more consistent. That is, your statistics can provide both close-up and wide-angle views of how your guidance policy is actually working and what needs to change. You can learn more about a specific child's behavior and prepare for a conference with his family, for example, while also seeing how fairly and equitably the program is treating children of color, children with delays or disabilities, and boys.

In order to gather this much data, you need an incident report form that asks for a lot of information about the child (e.g., age, race/ethnicity, gender, disability, home language), specifics about the incident (including time and place), antecedents, teachers involved, action taken, and outcome for the child. You can also compile other data, such as information about family contacts and mental health consultations. An example of a behavior incident form for a child appears in Appendix 2. In addition, you could create a special form to record observations of interactions, much like a running record.

The policy should describe how you'll collect data and state that the idea is to improve the program, help the children, and recognize patterns of behavior, not to evaluate staff (Schachner et al. 2016).

Exclusion

It is important to address the issue of exclusion in your guidance policy. Research shows that children of color, especially Black boys, are disproportionately suspended and expelled because of their behavior (Gilliam 2005). As a result, many states and school districts are creating policies that prevent early childhood settings from using this punitive disciplinary practice with young children.

In the words of the US Department of Health and Human Services and the US Department of Education (HHS & ED 2016, 2),

> A child's early years set the trajectory for the relationships and successes they will experience for the rest of their lives, making it crucial that children's earliest experiences truly foster—and never harm—their development. As such, expulsion and suspension practices in early childhood settings, two stressful and negative experiences young children and their families may encounter in early childhood programs, should be prevented, severely limited, and eventually eliminated.

Suspension and expulsion should not be considered for any child except as a last resort. Educators often fail to recognize small changes, so your input and presence in the classroom will be key before you and your staff reach this conclusion. Leaving the program is very difficult for the child and the family, so be sure that you have not only collected sufficient data to back up your decision but also developed a relationship with the family and encouraged them to see that there may be a more suitable program for their child. You should work with them to find a better placement, and to prevent the child from feeling rejected, allow him to stay until an appropriate one has been found. (See Chapter 10.)

For Further Learning

Book

Dunlap, G., K. Wilson, P.S. Strain, & J.K. Lee. 2013. *Prevent, Teach, Reinforce for Young Children: The Early Childhood Model of Positive Behavior Support.* Baltimore: Brookes.

Web Resources

Positive Behavioral Interventions & Supports (PBIS): www.pbis.org

Pyramid Model Consortium: www.pyramidmodel.org

Second Step Social and Emotional Learning Program: www.secondstep.org/early-learning-curriculum

CHAPTER FIVE

Enabling Your Staff to Act

As the staff struggled to find ways to address Andrew's behavior, it became apparent to me that their actions were more a result of their building frustration than intentional, thoughtful interventions. They were burning out and clearly needed my support. I began by helping them to recognize what happened when a child's actions hit a sensitive spot, then encouraged them to think about how their expectations and responses to the children were related to their own childhood experiences, to find ways to see small improvements in behavior, and to let me know when they needed a break.

Helping Staff to Understand Themselves

It's important for the members of your staff to think about the role they play when a child loses control and what they can do differently instead of simply blaming the child or the family. Some teachers will be grateful for the chance to self-reflect and will welcome any insights it yields, while others may feel threatened by the very idea. This is when your leadership skills are really put to the test.

The Amygdala Hijack

You know your staff and you know how you work best together, so it's up to you to decide whether to begin this reflection discussion at a staff meeting or one-on-one with each educator. Because the conversation might reveal personal information and push your teachers beyond their comfort zone, be sure to meet in a safe space and set clear ground rules (e.g., be honest, be respectful, listen to everyone, value all questions, keep what's said confidential). If you give some examples from your own experience, you'll make it easier for your teachers to open up (LeeKeenan & Ponte 2016).

Start by asking the teachers about the children's behavior that drives them crazy and why they think it bothers them so much. Remember, the same behavior does not push everyone's buttons (see Chapter 2). Some of the educators' answers may surprise you, but the entire staff must take every response seriously because it's a serious matter for the person involved.

Explain that a pushed button actually acts like a panic button: It starts the body's physiological response to threat—what's known as an "amygdala hijack." The amygdala, the oldest part of the brain, instantly judges the situation to be dangerous and activates the fight-flight-or-freeze response, which in turn raises blood pressure and the level of the body's main stress hormone, cortisol, causing an emotional, unthinking, and irrational reaction (Goleman 2005). In a little while, the rational part of the brain, the prefrontal cortex (PFC), will realize the situation isn't really dangerous and regain control, but if the teacher reacts to a child's behavior before her PFC can take over—while she's in the midst of the amygdala hijack—chances are she'll aggravate the situation rather than respond in a way that will help the child calm down and behave more appropriately.

Let the teachers know that they can hook into the thinking part of their brain more quickly in several ways: for example, by taking five deep breaths; by observing what they're experiencing, labeling their emotions, and reminding themselves that these feelings won't last (Aguilar n.d.); or by focusing on something that requires thoughtful consideration, like a simple math problem. If they take a deep breath and think "two plus three equals five," they will engage their PFC and override the influence of the amygdala, allowing them to respond more effectively.

Remind your educators that regardless of whether they're experiencing an amygdala hijack, any time they realize they're upset is an opportunity to role-model ways of collecting themselves. They can calmly say to the child, "I'm very upset and angry, and I'm going to take a deep breath and count to five before I say or do anything else."

Dealing with Stress

Some days, being a teacher or a leader is right up there with being an emergency room doctor when it comes to stress (Greenberg, Brown, & Abenavoli 2016). However, educators often find it hard to take care of themselves because the heart of their profession is taking care of others.

Self-Reflection

As you've just seen, self-reflection is perhaps the most obvious way for teachers and administrators to counteract stress. It's also an effective means of improving practice, offering them the opportunity to examine what they do, why they do it, how well or badly it works, how the children are responding to it, and most important, what they could do to make things better. This analysis enables them to make sound decisions and become more intentional in all their interactions.

Encourage your teachers to recognize how self-reflection allows them to bring information and beliefs from all aspects of their life to bear on their work—because a teacher's family relationships, schooling, experiences, and culture play a large role in how she initiates, perceives, and responds to children's behavior and classroom situations in the present. She might think back to how her family members expressed their feelings (anger, fear, frustration, sadness) when she was a child and how her adult self handles these negative emotions now (Nicholson, Perez, & Kurtz 2019).

In addition, it's worthwhile for the teacher to ponder how she was disciplined as a child, encouraged or forbidden to act, ignored or comforted when things didn't go her way. She might also want to think about her strengths and focus on figuring out what upsets her and what she finds calming. This thinking enables her to take more conscious control of her own behavior and to interact more intentionally with children and families.

Self-reflection is useful every day, and it's particularly helpful when a teacher wants to focus on a child with challenging behavior or when she has a disturbing encounter with a child or a parent and needs to figure out what happened.

Your staff should also know that self-reflection is helpful after an amygdala hijack. In such a situation, it's a good idea to do the following:

> Find time to focus on the event and remember as much about it as they can.

> Ask themselves what their body felt like. Becoming aware of physiological signs such as a hot face or a racing heart offers both a warning of what's coming and a chance to manage it better.

> Think about what actually set off their reaction. If they can identify the trigger, they might be able to minimize it or avoid it the next time. And thinking about *why* it's a trigger should give them insight into their behavior, allowing them to better understand its meaning.

Video-Recording

Another way for teachers to reflect is for either you or the teacher himself to video-record 10 or 15 minutes of a classroom day, focusing on his own practice (Schachter & Gerde 2019). Seeing themselves on video gives people a different perspective, and when the teacher watches the video later, he will probably notice things he couldn't see in the thick of things. This process can be very revealing and helpful if the teacher is open to it. To put him at ease, assure him that no one else will see the video. When you review it with him, concentrate on being nonjudgmental and look first at his strengths. Teachers who feel they're being criticized will be less willing to try out any new skills.

Journaling

Although journaling is a traditional means of self-reflection, it's often hard for teachers to find the time and energy for it. In fact, it can take just a few minutes and can just as easily be in the form of a text, an email, a video, or a voice recording as in a specially chosen notebook.

WHAT MAKES A GREAT TEACHER?

At a staff meeting, ask your teachers to do the following (Renard 2019):

1. Think about a teacher who made a positive difference in their life.

2. "List the top five personal qualities, skills, or attitudes" that made this teacher so exceptional.

3. Think about the teacher they liked the least.

4. "List the top five personal qualities, skills, or attitudes" that made them feel this way about this teacher.

5. As a group, identify and discuss any emerging patterns.

6. List the five qualities, skills, and attitudes that were mentioned most often and that they would like to either adopt or eliminate.

Teachers are more likely to stick to journaling and find it helpful if they devote a regular time to it. Perhaps they can make entries on the bus or at home in the evening if they can't fit them into their workday, and they can share and discuss their ideas with colleagues or friends if they'd like a sounding board.

The act of recording one's thoughts—what went well, what positive changes they saw in a child's ability to self-regulate or make friends, what could have gone better, what they would do the next time, and even what they want to know more about—increases self-questioning and self-awareness and allows teachers to keep track of the children's progress in addition to their own. Note that thinking about successes, such as responding to a child's aggressive behavior by waiting for him to regain control and then calmly talking together to find a better way to meet his needs, can reveal just as much as thinking about difficulties.

Mindfulness

Mindfulness is "the awareness that emerges through paying attention on purpose, in the present moment, and nonjudgmentally, to the unfolding of experience moment by moment," according to Jon Kabat-Zinn, an early advocate of the practice (2003, 145). He saw it as a way to train the mind, which he thought of as being like a muscle: With exercise, it could get stronger.

The core of most mindfulness programs is concentrating on one's own breath, usually by selecting a quiet spot, sitting still with closed eyes, and focusing on breathing. Inevitably, people's attention wanders, but with practice they learn to observe their thoughts, feelings, and sensations without judging them and are able to gently bring their attention back to their breath and the present moment.

Mindfulness enhances conscious control at the same time that it reduces automatic reactions like fear and anger that get in the way of rational thinking. It helps to improve social and emotional competence, concentration, and self-regulation and enables us to change ordinary patterns and gain greater control of our behavior (Cohen & Gonchar 2017). Patricia Jennings, who's been teaching mindfulness to teachers for years, sees it as the "simple ability to respond, rather than to react" (2018, 65).

Culture and Teachers' Expectations

One of your most important tasks is to help your teachers become culturally competent. Because challenging behavior often arises when there's a disconnect between school and family cultures, it is vital for teachers to know that "normality is culturally defined," as the anthropologist Ruth Benedict (1934) tells us.

White European Americans live in a place where people like themselves have long been the dominant culture, so White teachers are often not aware that they are cultural beings who expect others to believe, value, think, and act as they do. For these teachers, culture is unconscious—it is the environment they swim in but cannot see. But in fact, a person's culture is a product of her upbringing and surroundings, and as the United States becomes more and more diverse, whether or not someone looks like you, she is likely to have entirely different values and beliefs.

This is critical because as they grow, all children learn the skills they need to become competent adults in their own culture, and they come to early childhood programs molded by their own culture's customs, childrearing practices, belief systems, and ways of communicating and learning. That is, children's behavior reflects the expectations of their culture and family.

This is equally true of teachers, who also bring the values and expectations of their own upbringing and family culture into the classroom. Their cultural background impacts everything they do, including how they set up the classroom, their sense of aesthetics, their routines and schedules, and the content of their activities. Above all, it influences how they relate to the children as well as their expectations of children's behavior—and when what is appropriate in the child's culture is inappropriate in the teacher's culture, a culture clash can ensue.

Low- and High-Context Cultures

Researchers divide cultures into two broad categories, low-context and high-context (Hall 1977). The low-context cultures of White European America focus on independent functioning, achievement, and competition, and individuals usually strive to stand out by using logic and facts, direct eye contact, direct verbal communication, and deductive reasoning.

On the other hand, high-context cultures, which make up 70 percent of the world's societies, including those of Africa, Asia, Latin America, and the Middle East—as well as Native Americans and Americans with these same cultural origins—have a group orientation that prioritizes interdependence, being a good member of the group, helping and being helped, being modest, and fitting in. Their emphasis is on harmony and cooperation, so children from a Latino/a culture, for example, may happily share the crayons rather than expecting to have their own. Their communication is indirect and nonverbal, and they use the context to convey meaning—that is, they let each other know what they're thinking through stories, history, relationships, traditions, social status, analogies, gestures, silences, body language, facial expressions, and more. (See "Values in Low- and High-Context Cultures" on page 42.)

Educators, particularly those who are White European American, may know little or nothing about the cultures of the children they teach. This lack of knowledge may lead to stereotyping and misunderstanding on the teachers' side and to feelings of confusion, incompetence, worthlessness, and invisibility on the children's side. Behavior that teachers find challenging is often behavior that's misunderstood on both sides.

Values in Low- and High-Context Cultures	
Values of School and Early Learning Settings Low-Context/Individual Orientation *Example: White European American*	**Values of Diverse Cultures (vary from culture to culture)** High-Context/Group Orientation *Examples: Latino/a, Black, Asian American, American Indian, Middle Eastern American*
Teachers focus on independent functioning and achievement, helping oneself, standing out, personal property, talking about oneself, choice, and competition.	Families focus on interdependence and being a good member of the group, helping others and being helped, fitting in, shared property, modesty, harmony, cooperation, and consensus.
Teachers instruct by asking questions to which they already know the answer.	Children find it puzzling that teachers ask questions for which they already know the answer. Adults ask questions to challenge them or to find out new information.
Children must be called on and respond one at a time.	Children may not want to stand out from the group. Children demonstrate their wit and intellect by responding spontaneously and creatively.
To show they're paying attention, children must sit still and maintain eye contact.	Listeners join in and respond with gestures, movement, and words. Eye contact is considered rude.
Teachers tell stories about one event/idea, arrange the facts in linear order, and explain the relationship between the ideas and the facts.	Families tell episodic, anecdotal stories that shift scenes and address more than one issue at a time. Narratives unfold in overlapping loops, not in a straight line. The relationship between ideas and facts is inferred.
Teachers use implicit commands: they ask children to do something.	Families use explicit commands: they tell children to do something.

Adapted from Delpit 2006; Gay 2010; Gertz, as quoted in Kağitçibaşi 1996; Heath 1983; Lynch 2011; and Rothstein-Fisch & Trumbull 2008

Help your teachers to understand that their behavioral expectations—what they feel children should or should not do or how they should do it—are based on their own cultural values and experiences and what they've learned about developmentally appropriate practice (DAP). When White European American teachers want a child to do something, such as clean up the puzzles or join the group for circle time, they tend to phrase their request as a question: "James, can you put the puzzles away?" or "Won't you come join us at circle?" (Howard 2019). They often add "Okay?" at the end. Make your teachers aware that many children come from families or cultures where they are told what to do, not asked, and their response in the classroom to questions such as these is to assume that what the teacher is asking is optional—that they have a choice in the matter and it's all right to refuse—whereas this is not a teacher's intent at all. The teachers' phrasing may be so habitual that it takes a lot of conscious thought and practice to change it, but in order to avoid precipitating an unnecessary conflict with a child, teachers should put their expectations into a direct, explicit command: "James, please put the puzzles on the shelf." It's worth the effort because it can make a big difference in a child's behavior.

When teachers understand the expectations of a child's culture—for example, that she often acts spontaneously and expressively and jumps up and down or shouts when she is excited and involved—rather than assume the child is intentionally trying to disrupt the class's activity, they will be able to validate and appreciate her behaviors by giving her the time, space, attention, and warmth that she needs. Of course, not all children from a given culture act the same way, but it's important to recognize that there may be a cultural explanation for a child's behavior.

Even as teachers validate and celebrate a child's culturally influenced behaviors, they can also respectfully, and without demeaning the child's own culture, values, or behavior, help her understand and learn to meet the behavioral expectations of White European American school culture. That is, they can help her to become bicultural and learn to code-switch, or move comfortably from one culture to another.

In addition, leaders can help teachers to incorporate teaching practices and materials from different cultures into their daily routines, such as having the group respond in chorus instead of asking for individual responses. The latter practice may make some children uncomfortable and hesitant to participate, which the teacher may interpret as the child's not knowing content or not listening. Cultural disconnects such as this may contribute to the disproportional number of children of color referred for special education services.

Another example of a disconnect between a child's home culture and the program's expectations is the common practice of teaching children to get ready for outside play by themselves by placing their jackets on the floor with the hood nearest their bodies and then flipping them over their heads. When there are 8 to 18 children in a group, it helps if they know how to put on their own outdoor gear, and White European American teachers believe it's important for children to learn to be independent.

However, in some interdependent cultures, helping children to dress is considered a caring act that brings children and adults closer. Families in an interdependent culture may even think that the teachers are questioning the families' core values by teaching children to dress themselves. Although a teacher may consider a child's refusal to flip his jacket a defiant act, the child may conclude that the teacher who won't help him doesn't care about him.

This type of confusing situation can be resolved only by a discussion with the family. The teacher should open the discussion, even if she's anxious or reluctant, because she has been working directly with the child and should have already formed a connection with the family. You can empower her beforehand by talking with her about the importance of being open, listening to what the family has to say, remaining calm and polite, showing respect for the family's values, and making it clear that she cares about the child and will be sure he is properly dressed. At the same time, she must mention the number of children involved, and the fact that this skill allows all the children to dress and go outside more quickly.

Hopefully everyone will conclude that there's more than one way to do things—that at home we do things one way and at school we do things another way—and teacher and family will agree that the child can flip his jacket at school and his family can dress him at home. If the family cannot agree to this compromise, the teachers can help the child with his jacket. The other children, who are usually delighted with their new trick, aren't likely to protest.

Holding two cultures in mind at the same time in this way is difficult for both children and teachers. It requires teachers not only to believe that children need to feel accepted for who they are but also to broaden their ideas about who the child is and how the teachers can do things differently in the program. Both children and teachers need lots of practice, just as they would to learn anything else that's new and strange.

Social and Emotional Skills

It's also crucial to recognize that social and emotional behaviors are culturally based, and they may not have the same meaning for the child as they have for the teacher (see "Interpreting Social and Emotional Behavior" on page 45). In fact, the same behavior can have quite different meanings in different cultures. A smile, which in White European American culture signifies happiness or amusement, indicates confusion, embarrassment, or even sadness in many cultures; and what looks like timidity or lack of interest to a White European American may actually be politeness for others. In the White European American culture, eye contact is a sign that a person is honest and trustworthy, and to teachers it usually indicates that a child is paying attention. But to a child raised in other cultures, eye contact is rude, disrespectful, even aggressive, and to have a teacher—a person of great knowledge, worthy of respect—insist to the child "Look at me" must be quite frightening. Teachers who are puzzled by the behavior of a child should discuss it with the family to gain insight.

Implicit Bias

In 2005, research by Yale University psychologist Walter Gilliam revealed that Black children—especially boys—were being suspended and expelled from state-funded prekindergarten classes at much higher rates than were White European American children in those classes and children in K–12 schools (Gilliam 2005). Despite efforts to change this, children of color continue to be disciplined more harshly by educators than White European American children (GAO 2018; Office for Civil Rights 2016).

Research also makes clear that whereas White European American children are disciplined by educators for breaking well-defined rules, children of color are punished for misbehaviors that have no fixed or official definition, such as "disrespect," "excessive noise," and "bad attitude." Perceiving such behaviors as offenses is subjective and depends entirely on the personal judgment of the teacher (Ford 2016).

Gilliam suspected that something called *implicit bias* lay at the root of this disproportionality in expulsions and difference in treatment. As discussed previously in this book, implicit biases are automatic, unconscious attitudes and stereotypes that form over our lifetime as a result of our upbringing, daily experiences, and media exposure, and they drive the way we take in information, judge situations and people, and make decisions (Eberhardt 2019). All of us have implicit biases

Interpreting Social and Emotional Behavior		
Social and Emotional Behavior	**Low-Context Cultures**	**High-Context Cultures**
Eye contact	Indicates the person is honest, trustworthy, shows attention	Indicates the person is aggressive, disrespectful, impolite
Emotional displays	Open, spontaneous	Restrained, polite
Laughing or smiling	Indicates one is happy, amused	Indicates one is confused, embarrassed
Personal space	Arm's length or farther from the other person	When conversing, stand close or stand further away, depending on the culture.
Touching	A frequent and important means of communication	To be avoided
Paying attention	Children sit still and maintain eye contact.	Listeners join in and respond with gestures, movement, and words.

Adapted from E.W. Lynch, "Developing Cross-Cultural Competence," in *Developing Cross-Cultural Competence: A Guide for Working with Children and Their Families*, 4th ed, eds. E.W. Lynch & M.J. Hanson (Baltimore: Brookes Publishing, 2011), 41–77.

about social identities such as race and ethnicity, class, gender, and appearance—they are natural and pervasive. And they shape our expectations and behavior and influence us at least as much as the views we hold consciously, such as a belief in equity and diversity, for example. In fact, it's possible for our implicit biases to be the opposite of our stated beliefs.

In addition to our personal implicit bias, there is systemic or institutional bias all around us. In the United States, norms, language, policies, and institutions—including the health care system, the criminal justice system, the banking system, and schools—were established by White European Americans, so institutional biases generally reflect those common in their culture. Even the culture of early childhood education—developmentally appropriate practice—is based largely on White European American culture and influences teachers' programming and standards. Institutional biases affect people of all cultural and racial groups, often negatively for those who are not part of the dominant culture.

To discover whether implicit bias played a role in the harsh discipline often meted out to children of color, Gilliam recruited 135 early childhood educators and told them he was studying how teachers detect challenging behavior, sometimes even before it appears. Then he showed them a video of four preschoolers—a Black boy, a Black girl, a White European American boy, and a White European American girl—and used sophisticated eye-tracking equipment to record where the teachers were looking (Gilliam et al. 2016).

What did Gilliam find? Even though the children were actors and the video contained no challenging behavior, the teachers spent more time watching the Black boy, who they said required the most attention. That is, they expected him to misbehave *because he was a Black boy.*

In the second part of the experiment, Gilliam asked the teachers to rate the behavior of a child in a written vignette. He manipulated the child's race and sex by using different names—DeShawn or Jake; Latoya or Emily. The ratings suggested that both Black and White teachers had a stereotyped belief—that is, an implicit bias—that Black children are more liable to misbehave.

Implicit biases can go beyond the color of someone's skin. They can also lead teachers to expect more challenging behavior from children from single-parent families, families living in poverty, families with a home language other than English, families with same-sex parents, or families whose cultural norms and traditions are different from the program's (or the teachers' own) (Eberhardt 2019). When a teacher expects challenging behavior from a child, she is more likely to interpret his behavior as intentionally inappropriate when it is not, and even to provoke challenging behavior by the way she interacts with him. For example, at cleanup time, if a child from a collective, high context culture is playing with the blocks and integrating puzzle pieces into her creation, she will most likely put those pieces away with the blocks because in her mind they go together. The teacher might believe that the child isn't listening and may tell her to put the puzzle pieces back in the puzzle "where they belong." No matter whether the child quietly acquiesces to this request or throws the puzzle pieces, such an incident can lead her to feel as if *she* does not belong.

There is some evidence that it's possible to reduce implicit biases when we own up to having them and become concerned about their consequences (Devine et al. 2012). Encourage your educators to make this happen through self-reflection, increasing their empathy and mindfulness, and spending more time getting to know individual children and families and their cultures (Mann, Cone, & Ferguson 2015).

Because implicit bias inevitably influences everyone's interactions and relationships with children, families, and colleagues, it is vital for you to know about it and to support your teachers as they try to recognize it in themselves. However, implicit bias is extremely difficult to see and even harder to accept, so introducing this topic and enabling your staff to cope with its ramifications will require some extremely delicate discussions. It's likely you'll encounter resistance. Some of your teachers may refuse to believe that implicit bias exists, but if they do admit that it does, they may insist that *they* don't have it. In this situation it's important to point out that all of us—no matter what our color, culture, religious beliefs, or gender identity—have implicit biases and they often don't reflect our true goals and intentions.

Help your teachers to realize that implicit bias doesn't automatically disappear just because they are aware of it. It takes a conscious effort not only to recognize the bias but also to understand where it comes from and to become aware of situations in which it's affecting their actions.

A key strategy is for you and your teachers to work at self-reflection together, to admit that implicit bias exists, to name it whenever it appears, and to try to figure out how your own experience may have shaped it. Again, if you begin by sharing your own experience of how you came to recognize an implicit bias and the impact it has had on your interactions with others, your teachers may start to open up as well.

Another route is to suggest that your staff take the Harvard bias test, called the Implicit Association Test (Project Implicit, n.d.; test available at https://implicit.harvard.edu/implicit/takeatest.html). You should take it, too. Whether or not you and your educators discuss the results, it is important for all of you to recognize your own biases.

Implicit biases are most likely to show themselves in times of stress when teachers have to make a quick decision—possibly during an amygdala hijack. If in the moment a teacher is able to slow down her reactions, she may be able to control her response when a child's actions upset her. Otherwise, she might recognize later that what she said or did was not what she explicitly knows or believes. Teachers who practice mindfulness may well have more success in slowing down their thoughts, noticing their unconscious bias, and interrupting it before they act on it (Aguilar 2019).

Because research shows that acquiring new information about someone helps to alter an implicit bias (Eberhardt 2019), make sure your teachers get to know the children's families and learn about their lives and cultures, paying special attention to those whose beliefs and experiences are different from theirs. For example, finding out that a single parent is working two jobs, has no car, and can't afford extra bus or taxi fare may change a teacher's view that the parent doesn't care about his child when he fails to show up at a parent–teacher conference. Family engagement and home–school collaboration improve children's behavior at school (Ansari & Gershoff 2015), and home visits open doors, both literally and figuratively.

FIGHTING IMPLICIT BIAS

Can implicit bias be reduced with time and effort? That is the question that Patricia Devine and her team at the University of Wisconsin psychology department (2012) set out to study.

From previous work, the researchers knew that people feel guilty when they realize they're acting in biased ways. They hypothesized that if people know what activates their bias and have the motivation and strategies to replace it, they may be able to counter their implicit bias.

After the subjects in the intervention group learned the results of their Implicit Association Test, they were educated about the effects of discrimination and given training in five different strategies they could use in their daily lives:

> **Individuation.** They could look for specific information that would help them to see people as individuals, not simply as members of a group.

> **Stereotype replacement.** Once they recognized that a response was based on a stereotype, they could label it and reflect on why they'd chosen this response, how they could avoid it in the future, and what they could replace it with.

> **Counterstereotypic imaging.** They could think in detail about people who contradict the stereotype, such as a friend or a public figure like Michelle Obama.

> **Perspective taking.** They could put themselves in the shoes of a stigmatized person to see how he experiences the world.

> **Increasing opportunities for contact.** They could interact with members of another group in a positive way.

The researchers found "compelling and encouraging evidence" that the intervention reduced implicit bias and raised concern about discrimination (Devine et al. 2012). In a later study, the authors' findings suggested "that the . . . intervention produces enduring changes in peoples' knowledge of and beliefs about race-related issues," and these changes, the authors argue, "are even more important for promoting long-term behavioral change than are changes in implicit bias" (Forscher et al. 2017, 133).

Teachers can also gain new knowledge and discover a pattern in their own behavior if you find an opportunity to observe them or if they work in pairs, with one teacher observing the other and tracking and recording a specific behavior, such as which children she chooses to engage with and how she interacts with them during play.

Encourage your educators to make a point of connecting with people who are different from them. Suggest that they invite guests into their classroom, attend a service at an unfamiliar place of worship, or try out a café in the children's neighborhoods, for example.

As always, because each child is a unique individual, it's extremely important for teachers to build a strong relationship with each and every child in their class and to use every interaction to show how much they care and believe in her ability to succeed. A warm, responsive relationship with a child and with her family deepens insight and empathy and decreases biased discipline (Okonofua, Paunesku, & Walton 2016). Note that seemingly little things, like saying children's names correctly, can mean a great deal. Mispronouncing or changing a child's name insults the child, the family, and their culture and can have a lasting effect on a child's self-image and world view (Kohli & Solorzano 2012). So does judging children or family members by the way they dress or speak.

Arizona teacher Cheryl Redfield (2015) urges us to challenge our stereotypes about people who are different from us and "rethink, reflect, and resolve not to succumb to the convenience of overgeneralization." People can surprise us, she notes, and when they do, our horizons expand, our empathy and compassion grow, and our biases lose some of their power.

Using Data

Consistently keeping track of behavior incidents on a behavior incident form, as discussed in Chapter 4, will show you and your staff how much behavior change is taking place in both educators and children and will give you vital information about how to support your teachers as they work to improve their practice. To do this, you must make sure they understand that the purpose of gathering data is to improve the program as a whole, not for you to evaluate the teachers. (Collecting data is discussed in detail in Chapter 12.)

The more support and understanding you provide to your staff—whether it be to help them comprehend what causes them to lose control, to deal with stress, to better understand other cultures, or to acquire the tools to address their implicit bias—the more effective their interactions with children with challenging behavior will become.

For Further Learning

Books

Gay, G. 2018. *Culturally Responsive Teaching: Theory, Research, and Practice*. 3rd ed. New York: Teachers College Press.

Gillanders, C., & R. Procopio, eds. 2019. *Spotlight on Young Children: Equity and Diversity*. Washington, DC: NAEYC.

Kabat-Zinn, J. 2018. *The Healing Power of Mindfulness: A New Way of Being*. New York: Hachette Books.

Lentini, R., B.J. Vaughn, L. Fox, & K.-S. Blair. 2009. *Creating Teaching Tools for Young Children with Challenging Behavior*. 3rd ed. Tampa: Center for Early Childhood Mental Health Consultation, University of South Florida.

Mackrain, M., & N. Bruce. 2013. *Building Your Bounce: Simple Strategies for a Resilient You*. 2nd ed. Lewisville, NC: Kaplan Early Learning Company.

Samuels, D. 2014. *The Culturally Inclusive Educator: Preparing for a Multicultural World*. New York: Teachers College Press.

Position Statement

NAEYC. 2019. *Advancing Equity in Early Childhood Education*. Position statement. Washington, DC: NAEYC. NAEYC.org/resources/position-statements/equity.

CHAPTER SIX

The Power of Prevention

Even before Andrew left for kindergarten, we understood that another child with challenging behavior would inevitably enroll at the center. In order to avoid the crisis management we'd endured regularly with Andrew, we knew we had to prepare well ahead of time, and the best way to do that was to prevent challenging behavior before it started. That meant we had to take a hard look at our physical space; review our schedule, activities, and teaching methods; research curriculum programs that build children's social and emotional skills; and work at strengthening our relationships with every child at the center.

It's easy to bypass prevention as a strategy for addressing challenging behavior. Teachers may sometimes feel as if they're doing nothing when they prevent challenging behavior, but that is definitely not the case, because prevention is extremely effective. When an educator keeps a child from engaging in challenging behavior, she is not only making her classroom a safer, calmer, more pleasant place, she is also teaching the child a new, socially competent way to behave. In addition, she is stopping him from developing more serious antisocial behaviors later (Gatti & Tremblay 2005). Prevention strategies are especially important for children who've experienced trauma and need a place where they know what to expect and feel safe to express their emotions. (See Chapter 12.)

As the Reggio Emilia approach tells us, the environment is the third teacher (Biermeyer 2015). How can you use the environment at your school or center to create a caring, cooperative, and inclusive community that encourages learning; fosters appropriate, prosocial behavior; and, at the same time, prevents challenging behavior? It is the leader's responsibility to take on this challenge.

The Influence of Social Climate

Although the social climate of an environment is more or less invisible, if you look closely, you can see it—it is reflected in, and created by, the people in your school or center.

Larger than any one person's experience, the social climate somehow manages to tell everyone in the program which attitudes and behaviors are expected, accepted, and valued there, and it can certainly influence how people act. A positive, caring, welcoming social climate facilitates belonging and learning and can actually prevent or decrease aggression, violence, and bullying (Thapa et al. 2013; Zinsser & Curby 2014).

The backbone of such a climate is the teacher's warm, nurturing relationship with each child. Research shows that a secure attachment to a teacher in the early years not only helps children to acquire the social and emotional skills they need to make friends, exert more control over their emotions, and get along with their elementary school teachers (Howes, Hamilton, & Phillipsen 1998), but it also diminishes aggressive behavior (Hamre & Pianta 2005), reduces expulsion of Black children (Skiba & Losen 2015–2016), and may even help protect children from the effects of trauma (Perry 2014).

Help your teachers recognize that they need to develop a relationship with every child and every family in their class, to get to know who they really are, what they're good at, when they need more support, and when they might just want to be left alone.

As we said in Chapter 1, this process actually begins with you and your relationships with your staff. It's important for you to show that you care about them—about what they know, what they need to know, how they feel, and what interests them.

Talk with your teachers about what they can do—and are already doing—to build those relationships with children and families. How can they make every child in their class feel special, particularly the child with challenging behavior, who in her own way is asking someone to care, to notice the strengths she brings to the classroom, to provide her with the support she needs to start every day as a new day?

By having high expectations for all children, actively teaching social and emotional skills, using culturally responsive ways of connecting, developing class rituals, and giving the children lots of opportunities to cooperate and collaborate, teachers can create a safe and welcoming social climate and community.

MONEY IN THE BANK

Robert Pianta of the University of Virginia suggests these ways for a teacher to improve her relationship with a particular child:

> Observe what he likes to do and how he prefers to engage.

> Talk with him about his family, his interests, and his opinions about school and his peers.

> "Bank time" with him. That is, set aside 5 to 15 minutes a week to play with him one-on-one, letting him choose and direct the activity. The teacher doesn't teach or correct, simply talks in an interested way about what's going on, focusing on the child's interests and strengths and labeling his emotions. (Driscoll & Pianta 2010; Spiegel 2012)

The result of doing these things over time is likely to be a better relationship and less challenging behavior.

Try to catch a glimpse of the social climate at your program. What do you see as you walk around? Are the adults smiling and engaged with the children? Do they look as if they enjoy being there? What about you? Do you smile and greet people as you walk? Do you stop to ask how they are and how things are going? All of you together are establishing the tone for the social climate.

The Staff's Role in Creating the Social Climate

The first step in working on prevention is to brainstorm with your teachers about what's working and why so that they can build on their areas of expertise and feelings of confidence. Help them to recognize that they are role models first and foremost. Because the children are watching their every move, they must always be aware of how they relate to the children, the children's families, and their colleagues, and how their behavior, choice of language, tone of voice, facial expressions, and body language impact their interactions.

As role models, teachers and other adults have an outsize influence on the social climate. When they show they care by smiling, addressing the children (and adults) by name, saying "please" and "thank you," and speaking rather than shouting, the ambience is positive and friendly. Remind your staff that they should always be showing the children how to

> Express feelings

> Be sensitive to others' feelings

> Be kind

> Listen closely

> Offer and accept help

> Share and help others to share (Kaiser & Rasminsky 2017)

It's also important for the teachers to tell the children what to do rather than what not to do. Encourage them to set a team goal of trying to eliminate their use of "no," "don't," "stop," and "why" and to instead remind the children of the appropriate behavior ("Please keep your hands to yourself"). At the same time, urge the teachers to address the behavior, not the child; for example, when someone is throwing sand, their response should be "The sand stays in the sandbox" rather than "Stop throwing the sand."

Help your teachers to understand that it's important to eradicate the question "why"—even if they think it's necessary to understand the reason for a child's behavior—because asking a child why he hit someone or threw a block across the room implies that his action might be acceptable if he had a good enough reason for it. Depending on the teacher's facial expression and tone of voice, asking why may also make some children feel more defensive and emotional. Teachers need to understand that it doesn't matter why the child threw the block. They must keep the children safe, and throwing a block is not safe.

Rules

When there are rules, the children know that everyone cares about how they behave. Rules teach expectations, set boundaries for behavior, and help people to treat one another kindly, fairly, and respectfully. You should develop program-wide rules with the staff and expect the educators to do the same with the children in their own classrooms.

Three rules are enough. Young children can easily remember them, and with the teacher's guidance they can develop the rules and make them their own. Once again, the rules should tell them what to do, not what *not* to do.

The best way to introduce your teachers to this idea is to role-model it at a staff meeting. Ask them to work in teams to come up with three rules. First, like their responses to a child's behavior, the rules should be stated in the positive. Second, they should be impossible to break; for example, "Use walking feet" can't be a rule because it's sometimes okay for children to run or skip. And finally, the rules should be general enough to cover every possibility.

It may take some time for the teachers to go through this process, and you may need to coach them by asking "What's the first thing you think the children will say?"

They'll probably respond, "Don't hit!"

Then ask them, "Why don't you want to allow hitting?"

They will probably reply, "Because it isn't safe."

You can then say, "So 'Be safe' or 'Respect others' could be a rule—because it's a positive and general way to say the same thing."

Doing this with your staff will give them a better understanding of how to support the children in creating three rules, such as "Respect yourself, respect others, and respect the environment." For younger children, the rules might be "Be kind, be safe, and be gentle" or "Take care of yourself, take care of others, and take care of your school."

Once the children have developed the rules, teachers should discuss what they mean throughout the day and create a large expectations chart (see the figure on page 54) by filling in examples of what each rule might look like in each setting listed on the chart. Because consistency and family involvement help children to learn, consider sending the rules home with a blank expectations chart and the suggestion that the families fill it in with behaviors that work for them at home.

Needless to say, the rules will be broken many times during the day, and it will take time and many repetitions for the children to learn them. In addition to reminding children about what to do, teachers must be sure that any consequences they use are always related to the problem behavior. (See Chapter 11.)

Expectations	Rule	Setting				
		All settings	Circle/meeting	Choice/centers	Hallway	Recess/outside
	Respect yourself					
	Respect others					
	Respect the environment					

Expectations Chart. Adapted, by permission, from G. Sugai, "Teaching Matrix," in *School-Wide Positive Behavior Support* (OSEP Center on Positive Behavioral Interventions & Supports, 2008), 5. www.pbis.org/resource/school-wide-expectations-teaching-matrix.

Rituals

Program-wide, classroom, and individual rituals help to build community and a positive social climate by giving the children a feeling of stability, safety, close connection, and belonging (Howell & Reinhard 2015).

Sometimes rituals grow spontaneously from procedures or transitions, but teachers can also create them intentionally. When a teacher makes a point of repeating an act or action that always occurs at the same time or place and perhaps associating it with a song, puppet, stuffed animal, or the like (such as a cleanup song), it takes on a special meaning for the children and becomes part of their shared history, something they remember, look forward to, and understand—that is, it becomes a ritual. A good example is a morning ritual, which can ease the separation anxiety many children feel when their families drop them off. Because Mason had a hard time when his mother left, his teacher developed a ritual for him: Every morning she took him to the window where he could stand on a chair and wave goodbye to Mom as she went off to work. Then he was able to join his classmates and participate in the day's activities.

Social and Emotional Learning (SEL)

Social and emotional skills are just as important as cognitive and language skills, and they actually work together. In addition to assisting children to make friends and get along with others, they help children to do the following (Durlak et al. 2011; Fabes & Eisenberg 1992; Michelson & Mannarino 1986):

> Behave more appropriately

> Regulate their emotions

> Reduce anxiety and stress

> Achieve academically

> Make good decisions and reach positive goals

> Empathize

> Become more self-confident

> Resolve conflicts

Children usually learn social and emotional skills by interacting with the peers and adults in their lives. However, because children with challenging behavior lack these skills and are often rejected by children who are socially competent, they may not have the opportunities they need to learn how to manage their feelings, make friends, and be part of a group. Help teachers understand that children who are at risk for challenging behavior learn these skills more easily when they play with children who already have them (Bierman 1986; Strayhorn & Strain 1986), so it's important for teachers to help children to play together, to remain nearby to ensure that things go smoothly, and to intervene when needed.

It's important, therefore, to teach social and emotional skills proactively to everyone. Encourage your staff to find ways to integrate social and emotional learning into the curriculum. When everyone utilizes the same concepts and vocabulary, it becomes natural for teachers to model, use, and reinforce these skills in the classroom and on the playground. Because all the children are included and no one is shut out, the social climate grows warmer and more prosocial (Elias & Schwab 2006).

> The children in Andrew's class were constantly looking over their shoulders to see where Andrew was and what he was doing. They were waiting for him to decide where to play or sit, and as soon as he was settled they would find a place as far away from him as possible. The teachers rarely smiled or took their eyes off him, and tension filled the air.
>
> After Andrew left the center, we wondered how we could create a more positive feeling among the children and staff. Although some tiered prevention and intervention programs suggest that social and emotional learning (SEL) is just for children at risk of challenging behavior, we thought it could help everyone, and we started using an SEL program with all the children in the program starting at the age of 2½.
>
> To our amazement, by the time they turned 4, the children were clearly more empathic and able to solve problems without conflict as well as to build meaningful friendships (some of which have continued into adulthood). The improvement in our program's social climate and the decline in challenging behavior was remarkable.

Thousands of schools now use a research-based social and emotional learning program such as PATHS, the Pyramid Model, PBIS, or Second Step (among others; see For Further Learning) that teaches emotional regulation, empathy, and problem solving and gives children with challenging behavior a chance to learn skills that could make a big difference in their lives. With your teachers' help, do the research necessary to find a research-based, proven-effective social and emotional skills curriculum that they're comfortable with and will actually use. (All too often, the SEL box ends up in the supply closet or the administrator's office covered with dust.) Not all teachers want to use a prepared curriculum, and they should have the choice. However, SEL is most effective when the entire school adopts not only the program but also the attitude that SEL is important and there's continuity from classroom to classroom and from year to year.

The Pyramid Model offers a comprehensive framework for supporting and promoting social and emotional competence in infants, toddlers, and preschoolers. As a tiered, evidence-based model, it helps to build basic skills for developing nurturing and responsive caregiving and learning environments and provides intensive intervention for children with challenging behavior.

Its parent organization, the Pyramid Model Consortium, furnishes training, resources, and technical assistance to states, communities, and programs. (For more information, visit pyramidmodel.org.)

The teachers should show enthusiasm about this decision because their level of interest affects how much the children will learn. Fidelity to the program's instructions also improves results. Because children can't listen or learn in the midst of a meltdown, teachers must choose a calm time for them to rehearse and role-play the skills they're learning as part of the curriculum. As they put the skills into action in the classroom or outdoors, teachers should stay nearby to prompt, coach, and reinforce.

Some cautions, however: It's possible for a child to find the SEL lessons threatening and not want to participate. In order to prevent challenging behavior, your teachers should let him exercise choice and listen safely from elsewhere in the room. It's also important to remember that social and emotional skills are cultural, and they may not mean the same thing to the child as they do to the teacher. For example, for a teacher raised in the White European American culture, a child's smile indicates pleasure, but in other cultures it may mean that he is embarrassed. (For more about this subject, see Chapter 5.)

Physical Space

When you're considering how to prevent challenging behavior, the arena that's the least controversial and the easiest to change is usually the physical environment, which plays a significant role in a child's ability to stay focused, understand expectations, and build friendships, all of which influence behavior.

Talk with each teacher individually about her own classroom. Help her to look at the messages that the space might be sending. Does the room feel comfortable when you enter? Is it bright and open and child friendly? She no doubt has her own sense of aesthetics and probably knows how she wants it to look, so how does she feel about moving the furniture or the learning centers, removing posters, and limiting options for disruption—such as spaces that invite running or provide too little room for the activity they're meant for—without limiting creativity and play? Work together to figure out what to do. It's important to remember that this is her classroom, where she spends up to eight hours each day. She may not agree with your suggestions, she may have good reasons for doing what she's done, and she may feel strongly about her choices. Listen carefully to her views. In the end, you may need to compromise.

What's on the Walls?

It is tempting to overdo the decoration to attract the children's attention, but it's important to let your teachers know that new research shows it's wiser to declutter. Highly decorated classrooms interfere with children's memory and ability to focus, and those who work and play in them are more often distracted and off task and learn less than they would in a sparsely decorated room. Experts advise leaving 20 to 50 percent of the wall space bare, especially if the group includes children with learning disabilities or who've experienced trauma (Fisher, Godwin, & Seltman 2014).

With your teachers, go from room to room looking for anything that's potentially overwhelming. It's important to display the children's artwork, but wouldn't it be less stimulating if it were organized by color or subject? Pay attention to paint colors as well.

> We had painted each of the three classrooms in our center a different color and designed each with a particular activity level in mind—the quiet room for puzzles, drawing, and computer time; the active room for activities such as blocks, dramatic play, and sand and water tables; and the in-between room for games, painting, and small construction toys. The first act of our makeover was to change the color of the walls—we had painted the "quiet room" a very loud red!

The Noise Level

Research shows that a noisy environment impairs learning by making it hard for children to follow their teacher's instructions or hear the words of a story, so encourage teachers to turn down the music—and to reserve it for special moments (Sparks 2019a). Suggest that they arrange noisy activities like dramatic play, the water or sand table, and the block corner in the same area and as far as possible from quiet activities.

Visual Cues

Are there visual cues in the classroom that help children find materials or know where to go and what to do? These can make a big difference in the behavior of children who have difficulty processing instructions or understanding expectations. This is especially important for dual language learners who may not fully understand verbal instructions. Sometimes the solution is as simple as using shapes on the floor to keep the children from bumping into each other when they're getting ready to go outside. It's also useful, particularly for children who tend to feel anxious, to create a picture schedule featuring laminated photos of the children engaged in the day's activities and transitions so they'll know which activity is coming next. Children with disabilities may benefit from their own small, personal version of the schedule that they can carry around with them or that is a part of their assistive technology.

Organizing the Space

Although young children need lots of room to move, it can be difficult to prevent them from running if the space is too wide open or seems to contain natural running tracks. Help your teachers to arrange their rooms so that there is an obvious place for each activity and an obvious path for reaching it, perhaps taped or painted on the floor. For proper supervision, every inch of the room should be visible to the teachers.

Because challenging behavior often occurs in the block area, be sure your teachers leave the children enough space to walk around one another's constructions without knocking anything over. Space is also at a premium near the sink, so teachers should allow enough room for the children to wash up without pushing.

Sometimes it's important to control the number of children who can play in a particular area. Because the decision probably depends on the characters and cultures of the children in the class, they should help to figure out the capacity of each area, and older children can even help decide whether to control the number at all. For example, if play becomes too raucous or aggressive when there are six children in the block corner, they may decide that there should be a limit of five. The teachers can then place five numbers on a stand at the entrance and ask each child to take a number as she enters. When all five numbers are gone, no more children may enter. Teachers can use clothespins or colored cards to achieve the same end. (Bear in mind that children from some cultures may feel perfectly comfortable closely surrounded by their peers, while children with challenging behavior may need more personal space.)

There should be areas to accommodate small group activities like games and dramatic play, and even the computer and listening center can have seating for more than one child. The effect will be more opportunities for children with challenging behavior to form friendships, hone their executive functions, and practice social and emotional skills, particularly when they are supported by an adult.

Another way for teachers to cultivate self-regulation is for them to arrange the play materials so that the children can choose their own activities and supplies. (Remember, if they can reach it, they can use it.) Are there ample choices and plenty of the children's favorite items? The teachers should offer enough options so that every child's interests are represented but not so many that they create clutter and confusion. If teachers put some toys and games away now, they will seem new and exciting when they reappear later in the year.

Having a spot in the classroom children can go to for a break from loud or busy areas also helps them to develop self-regulation. Even if it's just a quiet corner in a noisy room, it should be furnished with soft pillows, some cuddly toys, and soft light. This can be especially important for children with challenging behavior, who may be anxious or have experienced stressful or traumatic events.

Welcoming Everyone

Do the rooms accurately reflect the cultures and languages of the children and community? Part of creating a welcoming and inclusive physical and social climate is making sure your teachers have and use strategies and materials drawn from the cultures of the children in the classroom. Help your staff understand that store-bought posters and borders usually depict stereotyped pictures of strangers, often from other countries, whom the children don't recognize or see themselves in. Instead, suggest that the teachers create a mural that reflects the cultures of the children in their group by asking them to bring in a photo, drawing, or artifact that represents who they are—their values, their culture, their family. Together with the children, they can then glue these items onto a large piece of paper or several pieces of poster board and hang it on the wall.

Likewise, instead of putting plastic food in the dramatic play area, teachers can ask the families for empty boxes and cans from the food they ordinarily eat. Furthermore, if a family member can take photos of a meal or two and email the results to the teacher, she can enlarge and laminate the pictures for the children's use in the kitchens and restaurants they have established (Nemeth 2019).

To make dual language learners more comfortable, encourage your teachers to pair them (if possible) with bilingual children who speak their home language. This can make them feel more secure and help them to retain and grow their first language, which is important for learning English (Espinosa 2010). As the dual language learners gain confidence, your educators can gently persuade them to partner with English speakers. Every classroom should be equipped with books in the children's home languages, and when a teacher reads aloud in a different language, she should first introduce the story in a way that interests all the children, then read it all the way through in the original language, rather than stopping to translate it page by page (K. Nemeth, personal communication). (Even when the teacher is reading in English, she shouldn't stop to translate into another language.) When she finishes, she can read or paraphrase the text in English. Teachers who don't speak a child's language have a golden opportunity to invite families into the classroom to read to the children, share their culture, and feel welcome as well.

Accommodating a Particular Child

Because every child is unique, it's important to prevent challenging behavior by considering ways to meet each child's individual needs, both cultural and developmental. Should the teacher move Benjy's cubby next to hers and closer to the door to accommodate his need for more personal space and less chaos? At nap time, is his cot too isolated or too close to his neighbor's or to temptations like the wooden blocks? All of these factors can affect children's behavior.

Making Things Run Smoothly

Curriculum and related activities, schedules, and transitions play an essential role in making the children's days feel safe, coherent, and predictable, all of which are key to preventing challenging behavior.

Curriculum

Because every child, teacher, and environment is different, it's crucial to tailor your preventive efforts directly with and to the people involved. Even when the state or school district dictates the curriculum (or if an early childhood center uses a curriculum like Conscious Discipline or The Creative Curriculum), leaders can always interpret and adapt it for their own setting. Encourage your teachers to consider this an opportunity to use their creativity. By looking at the most challenging times of day, they can shape the curriculum and provide activities that are culturally and developmentally appropriate for their group—which means that what worked last year may not work this year. For example, some children do best when there's structure; others flourish during unstructured, self-directed periods. Whatever program you and your teachers use or develop, it should take these needs into account.

Schedule

To a certain extent, the curriculum and the schedule are intertwined. Some children focus better in the morning, and the order of activities can affect their ability to self-regulate—for example, they may need an active transition, such as singing or moving, in order to shift from recess to a quiet activity or from free play to a teacher-initiated activity. Some children may even need a mindful, meditative type of activity to make these transitions calmly.

It's important to remember that everyone does better when the day follows a predictable schedule and the children know what to expect (or can find out by looking at their picture schedule). Has each teacher planned a balanced mix of quiet and active, indoor and outdoor, small and large group, and child- and teacher-initiated activities? Does each class have access to the spaces it needs? And have the teachers taught the children—and had them practice—clear procedures, complete with visual clues, for transitions and activities such as handwashing, lunch, and getting ready to go outside?

How much time and opportunity do the children have to explore the environment on their own terms? Make sure that your teachers schedule plenty of uninterrupted free play, because the bottom line is that undirected play is crucial to children's cognitive, physical, and emotional well-being—as well as to their learning. Through play, and with teachers' thoughtful support and scaffolding, children learn to manage their emotions, work in groups, share, negotiate, resolve conflicts, make decisions, pay attention, and see things from others' point of view, all of which help to prevent challenging behavior. Play also builds executive function and resilience, and new research shows that it even helps children to manage toxic stress (Ginsburg et al. 2007; Yogman et al. 2018).

Transitions

Transitions are especially difficult times of the day. With the staff, figure out which transitions could be eliminated and which need a revision. There are numerous resources that suggest ways to make transitions fun as well as learning opportunities (see For Further Learning).

The morning drop-off is one of the busiest and most demanding transitions for children, teachers, and families alike. Some families want to share important information about a missed breakfast or tell the teacher who will pick up their child, and many are in a rush to get to work on time. Teachers need to greet every child and every family, and some children are still having a hard time saying goodbye to their parents. In the midst of this hubbub, it's difficult for a teacher to give an anxious child some extra attention. But it's important to make this gesture a priority because when a teacher sits beside the child, asks some open-ended questions, and lets the child know that she cares, she may actually prevent his behavior from escalating and brighten his whole day. To enable the teacher to engage in this vital work at arrival time, you need to be present to help greet the children and their families, note who will be picking up their child at the end of the day, and assist those who need to leave quickly.

Discuss this situation with your staff, then send a note telling your families that the teachers will give priority to helping a child who needs extra attention during the morning drop-off. Families who want to talk to the teacher can either wait or leave a note. Ask parents to be patient and understanding: this policy exists because one day the child who needs special attention may be their own.

Teaching Strategies

Urge the teachers to use tried-and-true teaching strategies to help prevent challenging behavior, such as having the children work in pairs or groups, differentiating instruction, and utilizing the project approach. Your teachers can teach these and other techniques to one another at staff meetings, or you can free up time for them to see the strategies in action through visits to their colleagues' classrooms. Other useful strategies include splitting the group in two, enabling the children to make decisions about their own learning by offering them choices, using process versus person praise (see page 62), and engaging in mindfulness.

Two Teachers, One Class

There are times when it is best for all the children to be together, but there are also times when it makes more sense to divide them into smaller groups. When there's more than one teacher in the room, talk with your staff about which activities would work best in smaller groups and encourage them to split the group in two. This will reduce waiting time and offer children more opportunities to participate. It also allows the teachers to separate those children who may not be a good influence on one another as well as those in "love/hate" relationships. Bear in mind that even when teachers agree that this is a good idea in principle, some may resist doing it because, like the children, they like working together, and you may need to drop into the classroom to remind and support them. This is not a time to compromise or retreat; it's important to convince your teachers of the benefits and help them to stay the course.

ROLL THE DICE

To form groups that separate children who bring out challenging behavior in each other whenever they're together, have the teachers make a special pair of dice. If there are 10 children in the group, each die should have five sides. If there are 16, each die needs eight sides.

Each side should contain the name and photo of one of the children in the class, but the teachers should be sure to put the names of the children they want to separate on the same die. When they roll the dice to see who should be partnered or part of each group, the two children will never be grouped together.

Child Choice

For both teacher-initiated and child-initiated activities, it's important to offer choices suitable for every child's interests and abilities. Children often feel as though they have no control over what and when they do things. Providing choice gives them a sense of empowerment and can prevent challenging behavior. In addition, it's important to remember that children have different levels of ability and that if an activity is too difficult, they will do whatever it takes to save face and avoid it. Challenging behavior is usually the outcome.

> The children had all turned 5, and the teachers thought they'd developed their cutting skills enough to cut on a line and even cut out geometric shapes. They drew circles, triangles, squares, and rectangles on colored construction paper and put out scissors, glue, and a large piece of white paper. The children could cut out the shapes and create a mural by pasting their shapes onto the paper.
>
> Andrew quickly figured out what was expected of him, and he picked up a pair of scissors and threw them at Jeremy's head. Luckily, he missed, but the outcome was the same: After reminding him that it isn't safe to throw scissors, the teacher said that if he couldn't use them appropriately, he would have to tear the paper.
>
> Too late, we realized that had we offered choices to begin with—to cut out the drawn shapes, cut on the drawn lines, cut whatever you want, or just tear the paper—we wouldn't have put Andrew in a situation where he knew he would not be successful, and he wouldn't have needed to put Jeremy's safety at risk.

Circle and meeting times are often fertile ground for challenging behavior. Because there can be many reasons for such behavior, the first step is to observe and record what you see. Then ask the teachers' opinion: What do they think is the problem? Do their responses tally with what you saw?

Together, think about how this activity fits into the overall daily schedule and the children's needs by asking questions like these:

> Would it be more successful after nap or lunch?

> Does the content of the circle reflect the interests, abilities, languages, and cultures of the children?

> Is the length of time appropriate for the children?

> How is the seating indicated?

> Do the children have pillows or bouncy balls to sit on or something to hold in their hands?

> Does every child have enough space?

> Is there enough physical variety?

> Do the children need a longer unstructured time?

> Did the teacher notice the children were getting fidgety and realize it was time to stop?

You can suggest that the teachers make circle or meeting time a choice for the children and allow them to pick a quiet activity like drawing or reading instead. Even story time can benefit from this tactic and abolish a child's need to pinch or kick his neighbor, roll on the floor, or sit on his knees blocking the view. When he has a choice, he can opt out of the activity without using challenging behavior, and the teacher doesn't reinforce his disruptive behavior by asking him to move.

Teachers often fear a lack of control in the classroom. They may be willing to allow children to leave an activity but reluctant to let them return, if, for instance, they want to participate in a particular song or listen to the second book the teacher has chosen to read. Help teachers to understand that offering choices empowers a child by allowing him to figure out for himself what's best for him. It does not mean that the teacher has lost control, but rather reflects a more profound sense that she is in charge. If some of your teachers are skeptical about these ideas, talk with them about how making things work for a particular child will benefit all the other children. They'll be able to complete activities without being interrupted, no one will have to worry about their safety, and all the children will be learning and having fun.

Positive Reinforcement and Process Versus Person Praise

In the same way that punishing one child has a negative effect on all the children, positive reinforcement has a positive impact on them. However, teachers should be aware that when positive reinforcement comes in a tangible form, such as stickers or points, or coerces or manipulates children to act for extrinsic reasons rather than for their own satisfaction, the effect for most children is actually to decrease motivation (Deci, Koestner, & Ryan 1999, 2001).

Some of your teachers may not understand the differences between praise, process praise, and encouragement and how each affects children's behavior. Stanford University psychologist Carol Dweck has revolutionized the way we view these distinctions (Dweck 2007; Kamins & Dweck 1999). Dweck's research shows that process praise—that is, praise that addresses effort, the use of strategies, persistence, engagement, and improvement—promotes motivation and develops what she calls a *growth mindset,* or a child's belief that he can develop his own brain and abilities. Rather than engage in inappropriate behavior, children with this mindset are eager to take on challenges and see struggles, failures, and setbacks as opportunities to learn and improve.

In contrast, Dweck warns against *person praise,* which points at the child himself (not at his actions) by calling him good or smart. This kind of praise produces a *fixed mindset* in the child, or the belief that his abilities and skills are already fixed and he can do little to improve them. As a result, he hides his weaknesses, avoids challenges, and seeks reassurance. This outlook leads him to give up easily and makes him vulnerable to failure and low self-esteem.

Many teachers (and parents) have a tendency to use person praise in order to counteract low self-esteem and help children feel better about themselves. But this tactic has exactly the opposite effect: it makes them feel shame, which in turn makes them feel even more worthless (Brummelman et al. 2013; Rattan, Good, & Dweck 2012). Exaggerated praise works the same way, putting children under greater pressure to perform well and raising their fears that they won't be up to the job. These effects are long lasting and become worse over time. Process praise does not have the same consequences.

It's vital for your teachers to know that children begin to develop these mindsets at a very young age (Gunderson et al. 2013) and that they affect more than academic achievement: a fixed mindset also impairs a child's ability to see others in a prosocial way, behave in a prosocial manner, and resolve conflict and makes him more likely to approve of aggressive behavior.

Contrary to what seems logical, it is not necessary for an educator to have a growth mindset herself to promote one in the children she teaches, although for her own sake as a learner it is important (Haimovitz & Dweck 2017). What really matters is having—and conveying—the view that mistakes and struggles are normal and helping children understand that they can nurture the growth of their own intelligence and abilities.

According to Dweck (2015), even when teachers know about the importance of praising effort, they often forget to recognize the equally crucial use of strategies, persistence, identifying improvement, seeking input from others, and viewing mistakes and failures as helpful to learning. Studies show that educators have used the following techniques to foster a growth mindset (Haimovitz & Dweck 2017; Sun 2015):

> Teaching for understanding

> Asking children to explain their thinking

> Giving feedback that deepens their understanding

> Evaluating and praising the process of learning, children's evaluation of their own thinking, and any progress they make

> Explaining that effort, frustration, mistakes, and struggles are all a natural and useful part of learning

> Modeling their own attempts to solve problems, letting the children know that what they tried didn't work and they need to find another way to do it

> Working with children and sharing accountability for success rather than leaving it all up to the child ("Together we'll make sure you master this")

Keep in mind that the culture of the program also plays a role in acquiring a growth mindset. Children are more likely to try something new or difficult if they believe that you, your teachers, and all the other staff are interested in helping them learn and believe in their ability to meet new challenges (Blad 2016).

Mindfulness

Not only does mindfulness—the practice of being present and aware of thoughts, feelings, and sensations—help educators to better understand themselves and their interactions with the children, but it can also help the children to focus their attention, calm their bodies, build self-regulation skills, and even inhibit aggressive and challenging behavior. Mindfulness works because of its two-pronged approach: it improves conscious control while dampening automatic reactions like fear and anger that can spark challenging behavior and interfere with learning and rational thought.

However, for children who've experienced trauma, sitting still, eyes closed, in silence can act as a trigger, so they may resist mindfulness practice in order to protect themselves. But this isn't the only way to practice. Instead of closing their eyes, children can look down; instead of sitting, they can lie on their backs. According to clinical psychologist Sam Himelstein, one of the best ways to make mindfulness effective is to build an authentic relationship with the child (Schwartz 2019).

Practice is crucial to making mindfulness work, and children seem to enjoy it. Here are some basics to practicing it with children:

> Make mindfulness a special time. Move to the carpet or a space where everyone can lie down.

> Practice often—a few short practice periods work better than a single extended one.

> Select times you can stick to, such as after lunch or before math.

> Keep the sessions short. One to two minutes is enough for younger children; 5-year-olds can pay attention for about three minutes.

> Use props such as stuffed animals. Kids can lie down, put their stuffies on their bellies, and rock them to sleep with their breathing or pretend they're boats bobbing up and down on the waves of their breath.

> Metaphors are useful, too. Help children visualize their thoughts passing by like clouds in the sky or floats in a parade.

It's important for your program to be evidence based, so check out the research behind your choices.

Prevention is the best intervention. It is, however, often where you might meet the most resistance because it may require a new mindset and changes to the way your teachers are accustomed to doing things. Your presence in the classroom, your relationship with staff, and your understanding of the process of change will make a difference.

For Further Learning

Books and Articles

Charner, K., ed. 2005. *The Giant Encyclopedia of Transition Activities for Children 3 to 6: Over 600 Activities Created by Teachers for Teachers*. Lewisville, NC: Gryphon House.

CSEFEL (Center on the Social and Emotional Foundations for Early Learning). n.d. *Inventory of Practices for Promoting Children's Social and Emotional Competence*. University of Illinois at Urbana-Champaign. csefel.vanderbilt.edu/modules/module1/handout4.pdf.

Gelles, D. n.d. "Mindfulness for Children." *The New York Times Well.* www.nytimes.com/guides/well/mindfulness-for-children.

Hancock, C., & D. Carter. 2016. "Building Environments that Encourage Positive Behavior: The Preschool Behavior Support Self-Assessment." *Young Children* 71 (1): 66–73.

Jones, S., K. Brush, R. Bailey, G. Brion-Meisels, J. McIntyre, J. Kahn, B. Nelson, & L. Stickle. 2017. *Navigating Social and Emotional Learning from the Inside Out: Looking Inside and Across 25 Leading SEL Programs: A Practical Resource for Schools and OST Providers*. Cambridge, MA: Harvard Graduate School of Education. www.wallacefoundation.org/knowledge-center/documents/navigating-social-and-emotional-learning-from-the-inside-out.pdf.

Kaiser, B., & J.S. Rasminsky. 2017. *Challenging Behavior in Young Children: Understanding, Preventing, and Responding Effectively*. 4th ed. Columbus, OH: Pearson Education.

Salcedo, M. 2018. *Uncover the Roots of Challenging Behavior: Create Responsive Environments Where Young Children Thrive*. Minneapolis, MN: Free Spirit Publishing.

Web Resources

Al's Pals: www.wingspanworks.com

CASEL (Collaborative for Academic, Social, and Emotional Learning): https://casel.org

Mind Yeti: www.mindyeti.com/v2/s

PATHS (Promoting Alternative Thinking Strategies): www.pathstraining.com/main/curriculum

Second Step: https://secondstep.org

CHAPTER SEVEN

Why Change Is So Difficult and How to Navigate It

When I realized that our environment—our physical space, activities, schedule, even our social climate—had contributed to Andrew's behavior, I started doing research to figure out what we needed to change. What I didn't realize was how hard this process would be for some of the teachers. Some were excited about new possibilities, but others thought that Andrew's behavior had nothing to do with the physical space, their planning, or their teaching methods and that changing those wouldn't make any difference. Even though in some cases it was an uphill battle, the mountain gradually turned into a bump in the road as the staff developed skills to move gracefully forward, and the behavior of all the children, including Andrew, began to improve.

Recognizing the Need for Change

Change is hard. It alters roles and responsibilities for you and your teachers, and it's often difficult for people to think of doing things differently. Initiating and implementing effective, sustainable, systemic change takes thoughtful preparation. You must also recognize that it may not happen even though you see the need for it.

Sometimes a government or school board mandates change—such as an increase or decrease in required ratios, a new curriculum, or different rules for discipline—but it's more often associated with new research or an internal crisis at the center or school that makes it apparent that you need a better way to do things or even a totally new approach.

The project approach is a good example of how new research and ideas brought about change in many early childhood programs. "Directors who are successful in their administrative role view change as an integral component of a thriving center," says Paula Jorde Bloom (1991). "They see it as a continuous and never-ending cycle of identifying problems, exploring change options, and implementing new ideas" (22). The real challenge for every leader of a program is to bring about change that is sustainable and makes a substantial difference in the quality of learning and life for the school learning community—you, the children, teachers, and families.

Change is a process, not an event that happens in a day, a week, or a month. To a very large extent, it depends on what your teachers think and do, and it is more likely to take place and be effective when they are the ones who identify the need for it. For example, when one teacher at a staff meeting worried that the boys in her classroom weren't participating in the dramatic play area, thereby missing an important chance to role-play and understand their world, her colleagues chimed in with several ideas. With a lot of ingenuity and aluminum foil, within days the teachers created a space station—complete with a planetary destination, spacesuits, and helmets—that teemed with both boys and girls.

When the administration or the government demands change without consulting them, teachers can feel powerless, manipulated, and defensive and may well conclude that the new rules or practices won't serve the best interests of the children and their families. They may find it hard to commit to implementing the changes or consider them "the flavors of the month," and they may quietly block a new proposal without ever explaining their views (Johnson et al. 2014).

Why Do Educators Resist Change?

Some teachers will be on board immediately and feel excited at the prospect of expressing their concerns about teaching style, discipline practices, the daily schedule, physical layout, and curriculum. But you should also be prepared for grumbling and disagreements. Regardless of how small or necessary the change seems to you, some educators and staff will experience a sense of inner turmoil at the thought of it. Your job is not only to guide and ensure the implementation of the change but also to support all your teachers and help them understand and feel more comfortable about the need for it and what it will mean to them. Bear in mind that those educators who don't believe change is necessary and don't see any reason to let go of their previous practices and beliefs probably won't maintain any changes that they seem to accept initially. Your responsibilities include understanding why some educators are resisting. What are their assumptions, fears, and worries?

Most of us prefer the known to the unknown, and teachers are no exception. They have worked hard to become who they are, and they feel comfortable and invested in the current state of things. Some will say that they don't see the need for change, especially for a major overhaul, but it's likely that they're frightened by the idea that they'll have to give up tools and practices they've relied on, perhaps for years, and replace them with something new. They don't want to unlearn the old ways, and they're offended by the implication that the old ways were wrong or bad, even if they know deep down that they don't really work. The old techniques may stop a child's challenging behavior in the moment, but they don't really teach her the skills she needs in order to behave in ways that more appropriately get her needs met.

At the same time, teachers facing change may fear that they'll fail—that they won't have the skills or understanding to cope with the new ways, such as eliminating the impulse to say "no," "don't," and "stop" and telling children what to do instead—leading them to question their own abilities and diminishing their self-worth. They may feel bereft on some level, grieving for the old ways and for their own competence, relevance, and self-esteem, which they're afraid they'll also lose. Change will be especially hard for anyone on your staff who's experienced trauma (Bruno 2012).

Collaborate, Collaborate, Collaborate

Because of these concerns, a first step in creating change is to develop a culture of collaboration where you are the lead learner whose strong relationship with your teachers enables you to establish a deep sense of trust and to share power, responsibility, and decision making with them (Fullan 2016). There is more energy, accountability, and motivation when people work toward goals they've helped to set. And by empowering teachers to act, the leader becomes more influential and effective (Johnson et al. 2014).

Teachers shouldn't feel that change is being done to them, but that they're making the change with you. This is a time when facilitative leadership (see Chapter 1), which develops a partnership between you and the members of your staff and grants everyone power and responsibility for supporting all children, including a child with challenging behavior, will help you to create a common goal rather than divide your staff. Collaborative leadership gives you a way to understand the emotions your teachers are experiencing and gives your teachers the chance to share their concerns, learn about educational best practices, and discuss and reflect on what they're experiencing.

The next step is getting your educators to understand the need for change. Timing is important—you will have to determine whether they're ready for change—and so is data, which can strengthen your case. The need must be real—that is, everyone must agree that a problem exists and define it in the same way. Your behavior incident forms will help you to figure this out. (See Appendix 2.) Then it's essential to decide on goals together. This requires listening carefully to the concerns of each member of your staff and at the same time reassuring each of them that the change will be based on a shared vision for the program, that they'll all be involved in figuring out what exactly the change will be (Fullan & Pinchot 2018), and that you'll support them throughout the process.

When change feels personal, it can evoke an emotional response that makes it difficult to accept information and reason, so it's crucial to help your educators work through these feelings before you can expect them to understand the need for a different approach—or to implement it. Of course, each person will react to the change in her own way. But emotions are bound to appear at some point during the change process, usually early on. Look out for shame (a by-product of the fear of failure) (Berkowicz & Myers 2017a), shock, anxiety, anger, frustration, passive-aggressive behavior, eye-rolling, cynicism, avoidance, disrespect, noncompliance, helplessness, or some combination of these; and without judging the individuals who have these feelings, accept all of them as natural and okay (Aguilar 2017).

What Can You Do About Resistance?

The most important thing you can do to secure buy-in from your educators is to keep on listening to them, even if they're resisting the change (Berkowicz & Myers 2016). They are offering you insight into how they—the people at ground zero—perceive what you're asking them to do. Express empathy for them and let them know that their perceptions are valid and important. Consistently show that you have faith in their abilities to do what you're asking and be sure they understand that they're making a difference in children's lives. Change in attitudes involves values and therefore emotion (Bloom 2015), so be sure to pay attention to each educator's beliefs and values, culture, life experience, and priorities.

All of this work will require what Bloom calls "a delicate balance of providing direction yet suppressing the urge to overmanage" (2015, 35). So, for example, if you come into a classroom to observe how the teacher is using a new strategy and find a child sitting by himself apparently in time-out, a strategy that you've all agreed to change because it is ineffective, you must address the situation carefully. As hard as this may be, it is imperative that you do so—because if you don't, the teacher will feel free to ignore all of the goals and changes your team has forged together. There is no formula for how to do this; every teacher and every program is different. But it's important to try. The remedy may be more listening—more one-on-one conversations in which you attempt to help the teacher understand why she's finding this change so difficult and figure out how to make things work for her.

Because of their own upbringing, experience, and culture, some teachers may have very firm or long-held views about things as basic as how children should behave; whether children should always do as they're told; the importance and number of structured teacher-initiated relative to child-initiated activities; time-out, logical consequences, and punishment; family involvement; and social and emotional learning. If the children and families in your program come from cultures that are different from those of most of your staff, you will quickly encounter a variety of values and beliefs about how children should behave. These diverse views will probably cause conflict and resistance between families and the program, and you must remain aware that truly listening may impel you to alter your approach as you try to reconcile them.

Conflicts are opportunities to shift and expand our perception and behavior (Derman-Sparks, LeeKeenan, & Nimmo 2015), and borrowing, adding, and combining ideas can lead to useful new possibilities (Bloom 2015). For example, the recognition that a child who doesn't answer a question or participate actively is in fact paying attention and listening but has different ways of showing it should spur teachers to find new ways to approach her and assess her learning and behavior.

Many teachers believe that their job is to prepare children to succeed in the future: 4-year-olds should be ready to attend kindergarten the following year, 5-year-olds ready to attend first grade. This is why teachers sometimes argue that making changes that allow children to choose what they'll do—to leave or return to circle; to participate in a teacher-directed activity by cutting on the lines, just cutting, or tearing paper; to hop, skip, crawl, or jump instead of just skipping—fails to prepare them for the rigors of the year to come.

ADDRESSING CULTURAL CONFLICT

Louise Derman-Sparks, Debbie LeeKeenan, and John Nimmo (2015) tell us to tread carefully when change reveals a cultural conflict. They offer these suggestions:

> Be understanding of how hard change can be.

> Ask the teachers or parents involved to tell you more about why they feel so strongly and what you can do to make them more comfortable.

> Consider temporarily giving up a desired outcome in order to build deeper trust.

> Be ready to compromise. One or both parties may need to say, "This is the best we can do" or "We can live with that."

It is important for you to help your teachers see that having these choices enables children to avoid challenging behavior and learn self-regulation, confidence, and (hopefully) a joy in learning. And by the way, it is also enabling all the children in the class to have fun. Ask your staff if they think children are really enjoying the activity and acquiring pre-literacy or language skills when the teacher is constantly interrupting the flow of the story to tell a child to sit still and keep his hands to himself.

As you talk with each teacher, ask open-ended questions about her opinions and the problems she anticipates, then help her to reflect on them. You may be able to connect her with her own resilience by suggesting she tell you about a time when she tried something new, even difficult, and succeeded (Carter & Curtis 2010). Enable her to see the things that will not change and what she can control (Aguilar 2017) and talk together about what the program will look and feel like when you finally reach your goal (Bruno 2012).

Implementing Change

Once teachers have agreed that change is necessary, the vision, values, and beliefs of your program should be the foundation for any change and will help you to identify the skills and resources you and your staff need to implement it. Together, create an action plan. After you've decided on the long-term goal—what you and your staff are hoping to achieve and why change is necessary—follow up with several short-term goals that outline the transition process, which is important for ensuring that change actually happens. It is also vital to clarify each staff member's role in making the change a reality.

As you proceed, remember that this plan will necessarily evolve and that it must be flexible enough to respond to the needs of the children, teachers, and families that arise as it is implemented. As you saw in Chapter 6, it is often easiest to look at changing the physical space, to which teachers are probably less committed, before moving on to the schedule and curriculum. Changes that involve teaching strategies and responses to children's behaviors will probably be the hardest to achieve because teachers are so highly invested in them—but these areas are also where the most effective changes can occur. It is no doubt wiser to wait until your teachers are at least partially on board to start work on them.

Take Baby Steps

Introduce changes in small steps so that the teachers will have plenty of time to get used to them and start seeing some progress. Because it is crucial for the educators to feel successful, focus first on things that are already working well, such as the variety of choices offered in their learning centers and how those connect to the centralized learning topic. Then, if large group time is challenging, consider encouraging the teachers to make it optional, letting children decide whether to join in or to play quietly with a limited number of options, leave when they want to, and come back if they choose to. Coming from a position of strength will encourage the teachers to continue to implement the new way of doing things. When they're involved in making the decision to change, they feel more in control.

Provide Support

It's also important to have a support plan and professional development opportunities ready. Systemic change usually requires changes in knowledge, attitudes, and behavior. You can facilitate the process of change when you understand each individual educator and how she feels the change will affect her. Much depends upon the maturity and experience of the educators. When you're working with inexperienced teachers, you may have to guide them through the process or partner them with a more experienced colleague, but when staff members are qualified and have years of experience behind them, collaboration works best. What's most important is to talk with each individual staff member about the kind of support she'd like.

For educators who are worrying that they don't have the skills required to execute the change—those wondering "Can I do it?" and "How will I do it?"—professional development and change go hand in hand. Even when teachers are fully included in identifying and implementing the change, those with "limited ability, flexibility, and confidence . . . may become frustrated," Bloom tells us (1991, 39). It is therefore important to find appropriate opportunities for professional learning. While in-service training and professional development may introduce concepts, change requires regular chances for teachers to discuss, model, practice, coach, and support one another as they bring new ideas into their classrooms. This is most likely to happen when you've made your center or school into a learning community (see Chapter 8) that can generate knowledge and new norms of practice and support every teacher's efforts to experiment and reflect.

Take Care of Yourself

Engineering change will take a toll on you, too. As flight attendants say, put your own oxygen mask on first. Experts advise leaders to stop attempting to solve all the problems by themselves and give others a chance to try (Sykes 2014). As Holly Elissa Bruno puts it, "Letting go of trying to fix or change others is a powerful director's tool" (2012, 99). Make sure your support system is in good working order and you have the time and space you need to refresh yourself.

For Further Learning

Bloom, P.J. 2013. *Inspiring Peak Performance: Competence, Commitment, and Collaboration*. Lake Forest, IL: New Horizons.

Douglas, A. 2017. *Leading for Change in Early Care and Education: Cultivating Leadership from Within*. New York: Teachers College Press.

CHAPTER EIGHT

The Role of Professional Development

From our experience with Andrew, I recognized that we needed proven, research-based strategies and related professional development about understanding, preventing, and addressing challenging behavior. I had to work closely with my teachers to determine where they thought they needed more information and support. Together we could decide on the training and articles that matched those needs and figure out how they could share what they learned with the rest of the staff. We favored devoting at least 20 minutes of every biweekly staff meeting to discussing new skills and strategies.

Relevant, well-crafted, and research-based professional learning can ensure that your teachers grow stronger in their practice and continue to provide the best possible care and education for all children. In *A Great Place to Work: Creating a Healthy Organizational Climate*, Paula Jorde Bloom and her colleagues put it bluntly: "If you are successful at creating a vibrant learning environment for the adults at your center, then they will be better equipped to offer stimulating and engaging learning experiences for the children in their care" (Bloom, Hentschel, & Bella 2016, 58).

Being a director or a principal doesn't necessarily make you an expert in everything related to understanding, preventing, and responding to children's challenging behavior. And even if your expertise were unparalleled and you and an expert would say exactly the same things, your teachers still might be more inclined to pay attention to an expert from outside the program. This is where professional development comes in.

Begin with Your Staff

It's best to start with your teachers. They all have different qualifications, years of experience, interests, and abilities. Everyone's stock of energy and ideas is bound to run low once in a while, which means they will need and desire different kinds of professional learning.

The time you spend with your teachers in the classroom and the feedback they provide you will give you a good idea of each individual's skills, knowledge, strengths, and motivation as well as the challenges each faces. They are your partners, and research shows that teachers who learn in a collaborative culture become more effective at their jobs (Berg 2019).

At least once a year, ask your teachers about their long- and short-term goals, how they feel professional development can help them meet those goals, and what type of professional learning they would like to participate in. Choice is important, and there should be enough options in terms of content and type of learning available to meet all of their concerns. Together, discuss what would be the best fit and help teachers to select professional learning that will fill in gaps in their skills and knowledge and that will be compatible with the philosophy and practice of your program. Remind them that it is enjoyable and invigorating to step out of the daily routine, meet new people, and learn new theories and techniques. Professional development increases their self-esteem and job satisfaction.

Most teachers are looking for strategies to respond to a child's challenging behavior, especially those that offer a quick fix. Help them to recognize that no strategy works in a vacuum. They must begin by understanding the role they themselves play and the importance of their relationships with the children and their families, of social and emotional learning, and of an environment that prevents challenging behavior and encourages appropriate behavior.

Making a good match with your teachers' interests and needs is essential for getting their buy-in for professional development opportunities, and their buy-in is absolutely essential. If they feel that they don't need the training, or that their time isn't being well spent, or that you're interfering with their personal lives, teachers probably won't benefit from any kind of professional development. Those who aren't ready to learn will not learn. They will get the most out of any kind of professional development when they believe they need it, and new learning always works best when it has immediate practical applications.

A Learning Climate

You must also take the needs of the school or center into account. As the leader, you are responsible for creating a climate where learning and improvement are high priorities. That is, you must create what Bloom, Hentschel, and Bella (2016) call a "culture of inquiry" where teachers help to plan their own learning and understand the connection between that learning and the educational outcomes for the children they teach.

Model the behavior you want your staff to emulate. If you are an ardent learner who seeks out new information and doesn't settle for any old solution to difficult problems, then your attitude will rub off on your teachers. And if you're actively involved in a professional organization yourself, you'll set an example of caring about your own professional growth.

At the same time, treat your staff as competent thinkers and learners who are worth investing in (Carter & Curtis 2010). Make sure the atmosphere allows them to feel safe to practice what they're learning, to make mistakes, and to reflect on and learn from their experience. Let them know about upcoming workshops and speakers and pass around interesting articles—especially those related to your staff's problems and interests. Be sure to discuss the ideas and techniques they contain as a regular feature of your staff meetings.

Create a Professional Development Policy

NAEYC recommends having a program-wide professional development plan that works with your staff's individual goals. A policy can often relieve the pressure of having to decide who, when, and where your staff should attend a professional development opportunity.

With your teachers, consider these questions:

> Should professional development be mandatory?

> How will you determine who goes to which conference or workshop? Will the decision be made on the basis of need, interest, seniority, or other factors? Who will have input into the decision, and who will have final say?

> What if someone wants to do more hours than the time allotted?

> How will you as a group decide which type and subject of professional development is most important (Kaiser & Rasminsky 1994)?

> Do you have days set aside for professional development when the program is closed?

> Is it fair to ask your teachers to attend a training on a Saturday? Will you compensate them? Can they use their personal and sick days as training days?

Teaching is demanding. The job doesn't end when the children leave the premises, and educators may not want to give up their precious evenings and weekends to go to conferences or workshops. One way to turn these feelings around and convert the staff into enthusiastic consumers of professional development is to make both time and resources available for professional learning. Although limited time and budgets also play a role, your budget should reflect the importance of professional development. It is much easier to motivate staff when you can give them paid time off to attend conferences, cover their registration fees, pay their replacements, and bring experts into your center or school—but if you can't afford all of these expenses, it helps if you can spring for at least some of them, offer staff memberships in organizations like NAEYC, or find release time for staff to observe master teachers or one another (Bloom, Hentschel, & Bella 2016).

No matter how you manage it, it's important to find the time and money to underwrite your staff's professional development needs. Even for qualified, experienced educators, professional development can be an important affirmation. It is never a waste of time to learn new skills or have the opportunity to reflect on the efficacy of old ones.

Leaders Should Take Part, Too

It is crucial for you to participate in any training or professional development events that your teachers attend. It shows your commitment to them and makes supporting them easier once they're back in the classroom. There is nothing more frustrating for a teacher than to learn about a new strategy and find that the administration doesn't understand or support its implementation.

Take some time to think about how you'll support your teachers' learning once the conference or training is over. Research clearly shows that follow-up makes professional development much more effective and more likely to become part of teachers' classroom practice. It reinforces learning, reminds teachers to practice their new skills, and gives them opportunities to reflect on what they've learned, talk about it with their peers, and ask questions, all of which are especially useful during the early period of implementation when everything feels new and awkward (CDC, n.d. a; Darling-Hammond, Hyler, & Gardner 2017).

Looking for Professional Development Options

You can present the various possibilities so that your staff can decide what sort of professional development they prefer and the issues they'd like to explore in greater depth. The NAEYC website is a good place to begin, but you can also find information on sites such as Zero to Three and those of NAEYC Affiliates (see For Further Learning). Sometimes the best ideas come via word of mouth and recommendations from other programs.

Conferences

Conferences offer a great way for you and your teachers to network with others and discover that they're not the only ones working with children who have difficult home circumstances—three foster homes before the age of 4, a family member who's incarcerated, or parents who may or may not be documented immigrants but still fear deportation. Other participants working with children who are facing the same issues may share useful information and effective strategies. However, conference sessions are often short and may not cover your staff's concerns in enough depth. In addition, sending your entire staff to a conference is a very expensive proposition, requiring you to pay for substitutes as well as conference fees. Another problem is that different teachers are likely to choose different sessions, making it nearly impossible for you to attend them all. And such one-off presentations may not provide any sort of later support, leaving follow-up completely in your hands.

Full-Day Workshops

Full-day workshops can be effective when they're interactive and relevant and your teachers have follow-up support. Get recommendations from your colleagues and talk with the trainer or consultant before making a decision to be sure she provides high-quality, lively presentations, is knowledgeable about the topic, and is familiar with your teachers' supports and challenges. In addition, everyone should be comfortable, the room should be large enough, and your staff should be well fed and treated with respect. How will you follow up? There are several options: You can arrange interactive internet calls with the trainer during staff meetings, add extra workshops to cover problematic areas, hold discussions with each teacher and visit her classroom to provide feedback, or assign a fellow teacher as a learning buddy or coach (CDC, n.d. a).

Webinars

Webinars are an excellent flexible option because they can be a group event viewed during staff meetings or children's nap time, or teachers can watch them on their own. Several organizations offer and archive free webinars, making them available whenever you need them. (See For Further Learning.) You can use webinars to follow up a training, to discuss a particular topic with your educators, and even to find an expert to present a workshop for your staff or area. Although they're usually only about an hour long, they furnish enough information to engage everyone's interest and spark discussion among your teachers. Be sure to watch the webinar beforehand and make notes of issues to discuss and questions to ask the staff. Sometimes you can download slides or a workbook to help you facilitate.

Book Clubs

Book clubs create opportunities for teachers to explore new ideas and discuss the pros and cons of the information they've read in a staff meeting. You can select the articles yourself or ask the staff to share some they've found useful. Alternately, you can select chapters of a book, read the entire text, and discuss one chapter per staff meeting, or ask each educator to read and report on one chapter. Book clubs bring out personal stories and experiences, deepen connections among teachers, facilitate reflection, and help everyone recognize multiple points of view (Porath 2018).

Another possibility is to join your local college or university library. Ask the librarian to arrange a tour and instruction session for the whole staff. You could also create your own library by reading reviews and ordering books, journals, curriculum resources, and DVDs that interest your educators. Even with a small budget, you may be able to accumulate a range of resources. However, some teachers may see all this reading as an infringement on their personal time, and for others, reading may not be the most effective way to learn. Of course, the internet offers a tempting alternative, but warn your staff to be careful: There's plenty of misinformation online as well as information that isn't research-based or proven effective.

> ### EFFECTIVE PROFESSIONAL DEVELOPMENT
>
> In a review of 35 rigorous studies, Linda Darling-Hammond, Maria Hyler, and Madelyn Gardner (2017, 4) found seven elements that make professional learning effective:
>
> 1. A concentration on content, especially curriculum content
> 2. Use of active, hands-on learning
> 3. Collaboration in which teachers share ideas in pairs, small groups, or even with the whole school
> 4. Modeling of everything from lesson plans to observations to written case studies
> 5. Support and coaching based on teachers' individual needs
> 6. Chances to analyze and reflect
> 7. Enough time—weeks, months, or years—for teachers to learn, practice, and implement new strategies

Coaching

One of the most effective professional development options for adult learners is having the help of a coach (Williamson 2012). But be careful not to wait too long to seek out this option. If you've tried everything you can think of and nothing works, the difficulty is probably not with the child, the family, or the environment, but with the teacher herself—and that's the hardest problem of all to tackle. If she is at her wits' end and ready to quit, she will be less likely to accept the coach's suggestions and it will be harder for her to change her behavior.

Coaching isn't about providing solutions to problems; rather, it is about a relationship in which one-on-one conversations are intended to help a teacher develop specific skills and implement and sustain changes in her approach. The teacher should see the coach as an "effectiveness builder," not as a "deficit filler," says coach Elena Aguilar (2011), because she has to be willing to accept help and to trust the coach. As Judy Jablon and her colleagues put it in *Coaching with Powerful Interactions*, when teachers feel that coaches and others "see and appreciate them, they are more likely to risk a bit of vulnerability to ask questions and stretch their thinking and practice" (2016, xi).

The coach should be a trained expert listener who can assist the teacher in determining goals while at the same time paying attention to the teacher's underlying beliefs and assumptions, building on her strengths, and providing emotional support without judging her (Aguilar 2018). The coach usually observes the teacher at work in her classroom, then meets with her to ask open-ended questions that help her analyze and reflect on a specific issue—in this case, how best to prevent or respond to a child's inappropriate behavior. Coaching and the modeling that accompanies it enlarge teachers' capacity to reflect and apply their learning and compel them to accept responsibility for their actions.

Directors and principals probably have neither the time nor the special skills required to act as coaches, but many states and districts offer coaching at no cost. Check with your local resource and referral agency or speak to other directors or principals in your area to see if there's an organization nearby that can provide this help.

Mentoring

It is sometimes difficult to distinguish mentoring from coaching. Because both involve a high level of trust, the relationship is crucial in both, but mentoring tends to be less formal, with the mentor acting as an advisor, counselor, or guide over a year or two. (By contrast, a coach is more likely to spend six months to a year with a teacher.) A mentor is an experienced teacher who shares her accumulated knowledge with someone less experienced and provides important support for new teachers in particular, although mentors often assist during other significant career transitions as well. Whereas coaches usually pose a great many thought-provoking questions, mentors are more likely to field questions from their mentees and focus more on overall development than on specific problems (Lofthouse, Leat, & Towler 2010). In addition to helping new recruits learn the ropes, mentoring is an excellent way to retain experienced staff and provide them with the recognition they deserve. (See Chapter 3.)

Professional Learning Communities

Louise Stoll of University College London and her colleagues define professional learning communities (PLCs) as "a group of people sharing and critically interrogating their practice in an ongoing, reflective, collaborative, inclusive, learning-oriented, and growth-producing way" (Stoll et al. 2006, 222).

Backed by directors and principals, teachers get together on a regular basis to analyze and reflect on how they can improve their own and each other's classroom practice and thereby improve both children's learning and behavior

DOUBLE CHECK

Developed by researchers concerned about the greater rates of suspension and expulsion among children of color in early childhood environments, the Double Check preventive intervention utilizes coaching to produce very promising results (Bradshaw et al. 2018).

The researchers tried out their intervention in elementary schools that were already using schoolwide Positive Behavior Interventions and Supports (PBIS), and all the teachers in the study received professional development in culturally responsive practices. But the researchers found that compared to the teachers who hadn't been coached, the teachers who *had* been coached were significantly more skilled at classroom management, at reducing the level of challenging behavior in their classrooms, and at anticipating and responding to challenging behavior when it occurred—and they made significantly fewer office referrals of Black children (Bradshaw et al. 2018).

and the programs where they teach. PLCs have become very popular (Stoll et al. 2006), and in many places, such job-embedded learning is supplanting one-shot professional development events.

The overall goal of a PLC is usually to ensure that all children learn, and the underlying premise is that all children are capable of learning and that teachers will achieve this goal more readily working as a group, supporting and learning from one another and assuming collective responsibility. Using videos, case studies, observations, examples from other schools or centers, and their own experience, teachers discuss such questions as "What should children learn?," "What characteristics and practices are most effective in making learning happen?," "How will we assess children's progress?," and "How will we respond when a child has trouble learning?" (DuFour 2004).

The teachers' aspirations are their own, but they need your active support of their PLCs, even if you don't often take part in them. A leader can make the existence of a PLC possible by employing facilitative leadership and creating a school culture of continuous improvement and collaboration that respects teachers as people, encourages them to lead, recognizes that differences contribute to learning, and provides time for the PLC to meet during working hours.

Starting a PLC isn't easy. It may take years, and it will certainly demand that staff and leaders learn new roles, but according to Stoll and her colleagues it is well worth the effort (2006).

"Comparison of Professional Development Options," on page 80, lists the pros and cons of several common types of professional development.

How Can Staff Share Their Learning with Their Colleagues?

As you know, people learn from teaching. When an educator has been to a conference or a workshop that not everyone attended, she should be required to share the information and even provide a mini-training, complete with handouts, for those who did not attend. This gesture will help all the teachers feel that they're important members of the program.

In addition, attendees should submit a short summary of what they've learned and how they plan to implement the new information or strategy when they're working with a child with challenging behavior. Bloom, Hentschel, and Bella (2016) suggest asking attendees to share

> Two things they learned that they are eager to share with their colleagues

> Two terrific ideas they plan to implement in their classroom

> Two outcomes they hope will result from their efforts

Such feedback is helpful for the attendees as well as for their fellow teachers. It also furnishes you with a record of the professional development activity (time, place, presenter, and session title), which, along with your teachers' reactions to the activity and the content presented, will come in handy the next time you plan a professional development event.

Comparison of Professional Development Options

Type of Professional Development	Pros	Cons
Conferences	› Networking opportunities › Share information about what is working and what is not › Choice of many topics and presenters › Recognizing that others are dealing with similar concerns	› Sessions often too short › Difficult to attend all sessions that staff is attending › Follow-up required › May be expensive
Full-day workshops	› Can be tailored to staff needs › Are usually intensive and thorough › Opportunities for staff questions and concerns	› Hard to find good presenters › Follow-up required › Quality and value depend upon the presenter › Long day and staff may resent time spent › May be expensive
Webinars	› Cost effective › Available when needed › Can follow up with discussion › Can follow up other professional development	› Difficult to have the entire staff attend › Short and not interactive › Can be hard for attendees to stay focused
Book clubs	› Cost effective › Can be a focal point for staff meetings › Opportunities to explore and evaluate new ideas and information	› Not everyone loves to read › Teachers may see this as an infringement on their personal time
Coaching	› Teachers reflect and reach their own conclusions, therefore are committed to change	› Difficult to find trained coaches › May be expensive
Mentoring	› Helps retain experienced and new staff › Offers growth and challenge to experienced educators › Newer staff learn from supportive colleagues	› Takes time to build mentoring relationship › Hard to schedule time for meetings
Professional learning communities (PLCs)	› Teachers achieve goals by working as a group, respecting, supporting and learning from one another, and assuming collective responsibility › Supports a school culture of continuous improvement and collaboration	› Better to meet during working hours but hard to find the time

Your ongoing support is essential. You can never assume that because teachers attended a training they have the confidence to put what they've learned into action. Meet with them to discuss how they can implement their newfound knowledge, what they feel are the challenges, what supports they need, and what they want you to do. Ask them how they felt about their activity. What do they remember? What did they learn? Do they plan to make any changes in their program or their own behavior as a result? Help each teacher to develop her own action plan and provide her with opportunities to practice her new skills (Guskey 2002). In addition to whatever formal follow-up is provided, you should keep this new information in mind as you visit your teachers' classrooms and monitor their progress. Attending a conference or a full-day training is the beginning, not the end, of their learning.

For Further Learning

Organizations that Produce Professional Development Webinars (a Selection):

ASCD: ascd.org/professional-development/webinars.aspx

ContinuED: www.continued.com/early-childhood-education

Devereux Center for Resilient Children: www.centerforresilientchildren.org/home/webinars

Early Childhood Investigations: www.earlychildhoodwebinars.com

edWeb: https://home.edweb.net/webinars/

NAEYC: NAEYC.org/events/trainings-webinars

NAEYC Affiliates: NAEYC.org/get-involved/membership/affiliates

ZERO TO THREE: www.zerotothree.org/resources/services /webinar-professional-development-opportunities

Web Resource

Darling-Hammond, L., M.E. Hyler, & M. Gardner. 2017. "Effective Teacher Professional Development." Learning Policy Institute, June 5. https://learningpolicyinstitute.org/sites/ default/files/product-files/Effective_Teacher_Professional_Development_REPORT.pdf.

CHAPTER NINE

Facing the Reality of Challenging Behavior

Two years after Andrew left, Carmen came along. We had learned a lot from Andrew, but Carmen showed us that we still had plenty to learn about challenging behavior. At first, full of confidence, we felt that we had the tools to support her and work with her behavior. After encountering many bumps and sharp curves, we acknowledged that although she was only 3, she was in charge and her behavior wasn't going to make life easy for her peers, her family, or her teachers. Our enthusiasm waned, often to be replaced by anger and self-doubt. We couldn't seem to find a way to change her behavior. One reliable, excellent substitute teacher actually told me that she would be happy to come any day as long as she didn't have to teach Carmen's group.

The first time your program encounters a child with aggressive and disruptive behavior, you probably won't have all of your preventive strategies in place, and you and your staff will no doubt be looking desperately for effective responses to the child's behavior. This state of affairs makes it very hard to reassure the teachers and the families of the other children that you can work successfully with this child or keep the rest of the children safe.

A child with challenging behavior will point out every flaw in the program. Even if the other children seem content, this child's behavior will tell the teacher when the activities aren't relevant or interesting. Once it becomes apparent that a child's behavior is setting off warning signs, it's important to review the preventive measures you have in place and figure out how the staff can respond consistently to the challenging behavior. Take a deep breath, order pizza, and organize an emergency staff meeting. Then have a look at your leadership style and your relationships with your educators, the children, and their families, and review the changes you've made to the physical space, activities, and schedule.

What else needs to be done in order to support Carmen? Who could start forming a relationship with her right away? Which other child could be a play partner? Would it help to give her an extra personal heads-up about what's coming next in the routine? Remind the teachers of the need for self-reflection, the impact of implicit bias and trauma, and the importance of social and emotional learning. Review your guidance policy and behavior incident report form (see Appendix 2) and encourage the teachers to use them so that they can accurately determine the frequency and intensity of Carmen's behavior and hopefully see improvements, however small, each day.

How Does Your Staff Feel About Having a Child with Challenging Behavior in the Program?

No matter how well your teachers are prepared to address challenging behavior, they may be shocked when they actually encounter it. Some will feel they're well trained and ready. Some will be challenged and excited. Others will feel unprepared and unwilling to have anything to do with the child whose behavior is challenging. Still others will think they won't be able to teach the other children with this child in their class.

It's hard to get teachers to talk about how they feel. When a child's inappropriate behavior is pushing their buttons and the tactics they rely on aren't working, they may not come to tell you how frustrated they are. Even if you've developed a climate of trust in your program and your relationships with your teachers are open and honest, they may hesitate because they feel as if they've failed, and they worry that you will judge them.

Teachers may take a child's challenging behavior personally and go through a panoply of emotions. Don't be surprised if they're feeling everything from frustration to fear to helplessness. This is also a time when implicit bias may make an appearance and teachers blame the child's behavior on her racial identity, culture, or even her family.

Challenging behavior can make any educator doubt her own capabilities. No matter how many professional development sessions teachers have attended, some will still need your support when aggressive or disruptive behavior appears. At this point you must have a clear idea of what you want your role to be. It probably won't include having a distraught and angry teacher bring a kicking and screaming child into your office—an act that puts you in a very difficult position and does nothing to build the relationship between the teacher and the child.

Getting Your Staff on Board

Teachers who are already coping with large groups, endless paperwork, and personal issues need your support even more when there's a child with challenging behavior in their class or group. You are a role model. When you spend time in the classroom interacting with all the children, especially those with challenging behavior, you have an opportunity to show the teachers how to bring out the children's talents and interests and demonstrate ways to help them cope with their frustration or need to obtain attention or avoid an activity.

Caring Is Key

Teachers' expectations and their responses to challenging behavior are major factors in the way children behave. Help your teachers to recognize that they have different behavioral expectations and are comfortable with different levels of control (see Chapter 3) and that the behavioral demands of the classroom may be quite different from those elsewhere in a child's life. Children are basically resilient, and if they believe that their teacher cares about them, they will do their best to adjust to a variety of expectations and responses. The better the teacher understands himself and the potential risk factors a child is experiencing, the easier it becomes for him to develop a warm relationship with the child, find ways to recognize her positive moments, and give her support.

Early childhood educators are very nurturing and are often more aware of their shortcomings than their strengths. At the end of the day, they tend to share the times when they could have done better more easily than recollect when they made real progress. Try to promote a philosophy of staff ownership of the solution and provide opportunities for them to see, share, and appreciate those positive moments. You need to be in the classroom frequently enough to observe a teacher's responses to a child's behavior, provide feedback, and watch her grow. Part of your job is to understand your teachers' reality and support them when they're having a bad day. Help them to see both their own and the child's strengths and together work out a plan that reflects the teacher's concerns and her expectations of you.

Tune in to Your Staff's Body Language

To effectively support your teachers and provide them with the guidance and information they need, you must recognize what they are experiencing underneath the surface and what they really feel about having a child with challenging behavior in their class or group. Your relationship with them and your leadership style come into play here. Even if they don't approach you directly, there will be signs you can't ignore. Look at their body language—hunched shoulders, expressions of concern, weak and less frequent smiles, and increased absenteeism. You may get many phone calls on the weekends informing you that they won't be coming in on Monday. They may not feel comfortable talking to you, but they'll almost certainly talk among themselves. You may overhear them say things like

> "That child doesn't belong here!"

> "I don't have the training to deal with her."

> "Nothing I do works!"

> "I can never complete an activity."

> "I don't have time to give the other children the attention they deserve."

> "I worry about what her behavior is teaching the other children."

> "I'm concerned about the safety of the other children!"

> "She never shows remorse."

> "I can't predict what she'll do next; her behavior comes out of nowhere."

> "She's only three; I think we're asking too much of her."

When you hear these comments or get the sense that the staff is struggling to see a child in a positive light, it's important to bring their feelings out into the open. Talking about problems is the first step to solving them. You can speak with each of the teachers privately, but they may be more empowered and candid in the presence of their colleagues, so you could also use a staff meeting to discuss the situation.

The Children Are Watching

It is crucial to remember that the children are always watching how the teachers respond to a child's challenging behavior. What they're learning can be negative (challenging behavior brings extra attention; it looks like fun; that kid might hurt me; I should stay away from him; I don't want to be friends with him) or positive (the teacher will keep me safe; I can trust her; I can help someone who's having trouble; that kid could be my friend).

And although it sometimes seems as though the child with challenging behavior is influencing the other children, teachers need to keep in mind that the other children can teach that child as well. There is no need to make comparisons. Just by being themselves they are positive role models who demonstrate prosocial norms and values as well as appropriate ways to behave.

Should the Child Remain in the Program?

The question of whether a child with challenging and aggressive behavior should stay at the school or center will probably arise almost as soon as the behavior becomes apparent. Even if *you* have no doubts about keeping her in the program, your educators or the families of the other children may bring up the topic. In *Ethics and the Early Childhood Educator: Using the NAEYC Code*, Feeney and Freeman (2018) recognize this dilemma and suggest that once your staff have exhausted the skills and strategies they've used in the past, you should help them to identify their conflicting responsibilities (for example, to the child with the challenging behavior *and* to the other children). Brainstorm possible solutions, consider the ethical issues, and look for guidance in the NAEYC Code of Ethics. You're more likely to be able to keep the child in the program successfully if the family is willing to

seek additional expertise that could guide the staff's actions—from a mental health consultant, psychiatrist, psychologist, social worker, or school counselor, for example.

First and foremost, you have a moral duty to teach and care for every child at your school or center. A child with challenging behavior probably needs more support than any of the other children do. It's vital for her to learn to fit into society, and as trained and experienced teachers, you and your staff are well suited for this task. This may be the child's first experience in a group situation, and her behavior may be telling you that she lacks the skills to meet her needs appropriately. Suspending or expelling her would send a very strong message to both the child and her family: that she's bad; that she's unteachable; that there's something wrong with her. And when she enters her next school or center, instead of trying to prove that you've got it all wrong, she is likely to feel she doesn't belong and prove you right. Coming from you, a person

In the *Code of Ethical Conduct and Statement of Commitment* (2016), NAEYC describes the ethical responsibilities educators take on when they care for and teach young children:

> Childhood is a unique and valuable stage in the human life cycle. Our paramount responsibility is to provide care and education in settings that are safe, healthy, nurturing, and responsive for each child. We are committed to supporting children's development and learning; respecting individual differences; and helping children learn to live, play, and work cooperatively. We are also committed to promoting children's self-awareness, competence, self-worth, resiliency, and physical well-being. (7)

in authority who is supposed to be an expert in such things, this message may remain part of the child's opinion of herself for the rest of her life. For her own well-being, it's essential that you not give up on her.

Asking a child to leave would also send a message to the teacher. She would infer that you believe she lacks the ability and skills to understand and teach every child successfully.

What About Moving the Child or the Teacher to Another Classroom?

What if a teacher feels that she can't handle a child's challenging behavior and asks to be moved—or for the child to be moved—to a different classroom? When you talk with the teacher, you may find that she feels she isn't getting sufficient support from you, her co-teacher, or the family. Ask her what she would like to see happen and discuss ways to improve communication among the people involved. If you move either the child or the teacher, you will effectively be saying that you don't believe in the teacher's ability to support and teach this child the skills necessary to behave appropriately. You are also implying that she lacks the tools to overcome her own frustration and perhaps even her bias. Talk openly with the teacher about why you want to avoid moving the child and ways you can work together. You might also arrange a meeting between her and her co-teacher to discuss the problem and figure out how they can recognize each other's strengths, support one another, and devise new ways to work together. Let them know that you will visit the classroom on a regular basis to observe the child, suggest how they can prevent her difficult behavior, and offer them ideas about how to respond should it occur.

Remember that there can be incidents where the teacher is worrying not only about the safety of the other children but also about her own well-being. Even if she handled things well, it's possible that the child's behavior has triggered an emotional response in her, and when our buttons are pushed and our amygdala takes over, we often need some time to pull ourselves together. If there is no extra staff, offer to spend some time in her classroom to give her a break.

Supporting Teachers When There's a Child with Challenging Behavior

There are obviously many ways for you to be involved. Some teachers may feel that asking for help is a sign of failure and will try to deescalate the child's behavior on their own. Others may just want the child to leave their classroom, and your office is the most obvious spot to put him. Or, regardless of the work you and the staff have done, the educator is still resorting to time-out, which will stop the behavior but not change it. Still others want to intimidate or scare the child into behaving in a particular way and are using your office as a threat. They think the child regards an office visit as a punishment, but it's more likely that they're saying they can no longer cope and they actually mean "I can't do this anymore. He's ruining the activity and hurting other kids." Before they reach the end of their rope, you and the staff must discuss the pros and cons of possible actions and decide which ones will best meet everyone's needs.

Being There

Although you have numerous other things to do, when there's trouble and a teacher needs or asks for your help, you should go to the classroom. If you ordinarily spend time with the children there, your arrival probably won't change the scenario. Your job is to work with the group and enable the teacher to focus on the child with challenging behavior in order to show her (and all the other children) that the teacher knows what to do. When the educator is prepared and knows how to respond effectively to a child who's out of control, her actions can cement the teacher–child relationship, lessen the anxiety and fear of the other children in the group, and make the educator herself feel more effective.

On the other hand, if you interfere or engage with the child, all of the children, including the child with challenging behavior, will think that the teacher cannot handle the situation or that she doesn't care about this child. If you consider the risk factors that many children with challenging behavior face, such as trauma or attachment issues, it becomes clear that building a relationship with the child can be more effective than zeroing in on the behavior itself. Remind the teacher that if she concentrates on establishing a relationship with every child, including the ones with challenging behavior, the behavior will decrease. Children don't care unless they think their teacher cares.

Role-Model a Response

For many educators, addressing challenging behavior can be a difficult task, and it is particularly hard for those who lack training and life experience. They may not know how to identify the child's needs or realize that a hug would be more helpful than a punishment, especially after the child has kicked or spat on them. If you witness a situation in which you feel that a teacher may be doing more harm than good, you can use it as an opportunity to role-model an appropriate response. But afterward, be sure to let her know what you were doing by saying explicitly, "I wasn't trying to take over, but I thought this was a good time to model what can be done. Do you feel confident enough to try engaging with the child next time?"

Talk with the teacher privately as soon after the incident as possible. If you have an extra staff member, ask her to replace the teacher in the classroom. If this isn't possible, carve out some time during her lunch break or after her shift. It's important to start on a positive note—the fact that the child is now calm and everyone is safe. Follow up with a discussion of how the educator feels about the incident. What does she know about the child's life and the risk and protective factors she faces every day? What does she think provoked the behavior? What might be happening in the child's life that precipitated her actions? What was the child communicating? How does the teacher feel about her own participation in the situation?

When you work with the teacher, you are letting her know that this experience will enable her to become a better teacher. Therefore, as hard as it might be, it is important to provide the support and information she needs in order to change her feelings about this child and increase her ability to assist her and any other children in the future. If she becomes defensive, don't take her attitude personally. Let her know that you understand it wasn't easy for her to be honest with you and you appreciate it. Encourage her to take on the responsibility of identifying which skills and training she needs in order to respond more effectively when a child is out of control. What can she do to prevent the behavior from occurring again? How does she think you can support her?

Help the Teacher Find the Child's Strengths

A deficit perspective focuses on what the child can't do and why she doesn't fit in. Instead, help the teacher to see the child's strengths. What *can* she do? What does she like to do? When does she behave appropriately? The teacher must always think of the child's needs as she prepares lessons, arranges the classroom, and interacts with the children. If she can make the program work for Carmen, if she can offer activities that reflect Carmen's interests and abilities, everyone will benefit. Describing a child as "having difficulty with" a given behavior makes it clear that teaching needed skills is the best response. It will help your educators to recognize that their job is to teach if they see that a child who screams or throws things needs to learn better ways to attract their attention.

Work with the Family

If the discussion leads the educator to blame the family for the child's behavior ("No one is setting limits at home!," "She gets to do whatever she wants," "Mom just drops her off without saying good-bye or even talking to her at all," and "She's always the last to be picked up"), it's important to remind her that the parents are doing their best. As hard as it may be, she needs to develop a relationship with the family so that they can work together. Explain that the teacher cannot change the child's life, but she can help by providing opportunities for her to succeed at school. (See Chapter 10 for more about working with families.)

Focus on the Classroom

In the meantime, observe what's happening in the classroom. If possible, try to be present when the children are arriving because that early morning start reveals so much about how the day will go. How is the teacher greeting each child and what has she done to help all the children feel more comfortable and settle into the classroom? Did Carmen cling to her mother at drop-off? Did she have difficulty making eye contact with the teacher or her peers and then choose to play by herself?

Take a look around the classroom, observe activities, and go over lesson plans. Has the teacher made any changes to prevent the child's challenging behavior? How does she respond when Carmen's behavior becomes disruptive or aggressive and when her behavior is appropriate? Think about how you can help her notice and pay attention when she's behaving appropriately and reinforce what she's doing right. Remind her of this often-quoted wisdom from Tom Herner, former president of the National Association of State Directors of Special Education (1998):

> If a child doesn't know how to read, we teach.
> If a child doesn't know how to swim, we teach.
> If a child doesn't know how to multiply, we teach.
> If a child doesn't know how to drive, we teach.
> If a child doesn't know how to behave, we . . . punish?
>
> Why can't we finish the last sentence as automatically as we do the others?

How Can Staff Meetings Help?

If a child's teacher is comfortable with the idea, it may be helpful to have an open discussion with the entire staff. Her colleagues may contribute positive insights and ideas that help them all to address challenging behavior. But don't let this meeting degenerate into a complaint session that jeopardizes your ability to work together in a positive way; concentrate instead on helping the educators to see the child's strengths and recognize how she will make them better teachers. They must remember that this is neither the first nor the last child who will challenge them.

Staff meetings are only as useful as the staff perceives them to be. Margie Carter and Deb Curtis (2010) regard them as a time to share, reflect, strengthen relationships, and build a sense of belonging. But they are also a time for enhancing professional development, and they furnish an important chance for people to discuss their experiences and points of view about individual children and problems. They are especially useful when a staff member wants to tell her colleagues about her success with a child with challenging behavior; when someone feels strongly that you haven't provided her with enough support; or when a teacher believes that a child should be asked to leave the program. Staff meetings can help teachers own the problem-solving process as well as the solutions to the problem.

When scheduling a staff meeting, be sure to find out when it is most convenient for all members of your staff to attend. Although most schools block out times for staff meetings, scheduling is a perpetual problem for early childhood centers. Many educators work in shifts, so a meeting at the end of the day might require them to remain at the center after they've finished working. You could pay them for the extra hours, but the day is very long and they may just want to go home. It's possible to meet during nap time if you can call in additional staff to watch the children. Alternately, you could recruit parent volunteers or qualified students, provided your licensing and board rules permit it. Evenings are another possibility if you can supply food and transportation, but once your teachers have arrived home they may not wish to return to the school or it may not be feasible for them to do so. Nonetheless, it is essential to work out a time and hold these meetings.

Enable the teachers to participate in creating the agenda. You can do this on a board or chart paper in the staff room or ask each educator to provide one or more items she wants to discuss. Your role is to prioritize the issues and figure out how much time your teachers need to open up and feel comfortable sharing their concerns. To give them more power and responsibility and boost their involvement with the issues, you could suggest they take over chairing the meetings, perhaps in rotation.

Don't leave them hanging after an issue has been discussed. They have been forthright and willing to speak out, so before you move on, be sure that you've created a plan that everyone feels comfortable trying. This is also a time to share articles, conference handouts, and take-home messages from the workshops they've attended. Help the teachers to connect their daily classroom practice with what they've learned. Talk with them about what makes this process hard and how you can facilitate this link for them.

When Is It Time to Call in Reinforcements?

Before you call in an expert to help your overwhelmed teachers, you might consider engaging another person, even just part-time, to offer extra support. Discuss this idea with the entire staff. What would they want this person's role to be? Are there particular times of the day when additional support would help things to run more smoothly?

Another alternative is to request a mental health consultation or coaching. Many states and school districts now provide these services to early childhood centers and school classrooms, often for free. Before you decide to go this route, check the regulations regarding the need to inform or request permission from the family. Every state, district, and school board has its own rules. Some consider coaching to be focused on the teacher, not the child; and if the mental health consultant is a member of the Department of Education or the school staff, parental permission may not be necessary. But in other situations, written permission is required before any professional can observe a child.

The consultants—who usually hold a master's degree in the mental health field, social work, or education—also have a deep knowledge of child development, early childhood mental health, early childhood settings, and community resources. They don't work directly with children; rather they partner with teachers, observing, training, coaching, and modeling as they build the teachers' capacity to support children's social and emotional development and prevent and reduce challenging behavior. Customized to fit each situation, their work may focus on a single child, a family, or a whole program (Hepburn et al. 2013).

Research shows that early childhood mental health consultation can

> Reduce challenging behavior

> Prevent suspension and expulsion

> Improve classroom climate

> Strengthen teacher–child interactions

> Enhance children's social and emotional skills and positive behavior

> Boost teachers' confidence in their ability to address children's needs and challenging behavior

> Reduce staff stress, burnout, and turnover

> Improve communication between parents and teachers and lessen parents' stress (Duran et al., n.d.; Gilliam 2005; Gilliam 2007; Hepburn et al. 2013)

Because consultants are often in short supply, it may be hard to find one, and you will probably be responsible for recruitment. Look for someone who's a good match for the needs and philosophy of your program and introduce her to your staff and families as soon as possible. If they're going to accept any advice or suggestions, it's crucial for them to understand that the consultant is there not to monitor or judge but to help and support them (Duran et al., n.d.).

Arranging for a mental health consultant is just the first step. The second step is to help the teacher understand the advice she is given and support her efforts to make some of the suggested changes.

BOOSTING COLLABORATION

Here are some tips for creating effective collaboration among teachers, consultants, and families (Duran et al., n.d., as adapted from Green et al., n.d.):

> Give your consultant an orientation to your school or program.

> Be sure that your staff understands the role of the consultant and when, how, and what services he or she will provide.

> While protecting confidentiality, encourage the consultant and your teachers and parents to share information.

> Give staff direct email or phone access to the consultant.

> Schedule regular times for the consultant to be in classrooms.

> Ask the consultant to attend meetings where staff discuss specific children and families.

> If possible, maintain a relationship with your consultant over time so that he or she is seen as part of your team.

Regardless of what you decide to do, don't put off getting assistance. The longer the child engages in inappropriate behavior to meet her needs, the harder it becomes to change that behavior. And if you wait until your teachers are on the verge of burnout, they may not feel relieved that you've called in an expert or hired more staff. In fact, they may resent it, ignore the expert's advice, and complain to you and each other that they, too, would have no problem if all they had to do was make sure the child with challenging behavior participated appropriately. Even if this added support improves the classroom climate and the child's behavior, some teachers may become defensive and regard the other's presence as an indication of their own shortcomings.

Throughout this entire process, you must stay calm. You may not always like or agree with what you hear, but you must always remember that you need to care for the people who care for the children.

For Further Learning

Books

Feeney, S., & N.K. Freeman. 2018. *Ethics and the Early Childhood Educator: Using the NAEYC Code.* 3rd ed. Washington, DC: NAEYC.

Kaiser, B., & J.S. Rasminsky. 2017. *Challenging Behavior in Young Children: Understanding, Preventing, and Responding Effectively.* 4th ed. Columbus, OH: Pearson Education.

Position Statement

NAEYC. 2011. "Code of Ethical Conduct and Statement of Commitment." Position statement. NAEYC.org/files/naeyc/file/positions/PSETH05.pdf.

CHAPTER TEN
Working with the Family

Carmen's mother was a single parent who was not only attending university at night but also holding down a full-time job at a factory. She was exhausted when she came to pick up her child. The last thing she needed to hear was how Carmen was climbing on shelves, grabbing toys from others, and yelling at the top of her lungs. Carmen had trouble with transitions; when her mother arrived, she would often scream, throw things, and run off. I would join Carmen's mother and role-model ways to help Carmen get ready to go home.

Our work with Carmen—helping her learn to use her strengths, like her quick mind and her eagerness to make friends—was beginning to reap rewards, so we were able to tell her mother about the new friends she had made and her painting that was on the wall. We suggested she take a few minutes to sit with Carmen and ask about her day before they got ready for the journey home. Over time, Carmen seemed to be more prepared to leave, and simultaneously her mother started to notice changes in her behavior at home. One day she made a point of asking us about what we were doing so that she could use the same strategies. With her mother's support, we stayed on track. Carmen became cooperative, followed instructions, and engaged appropriately with her peers.

As the authors of *Families and Educators Together* tell us, "When you work with young children, you work with their families as well. . . . Together, you support the healthy development and learning of each child" (Koralek, Nemeth, & Ramsey 2019, 1). In entrusting you and your educators with the task of caring for their child, families are handing over the most precious person in their lives to complete strangers. Once families enroll, it is imperative for you and your teachers to start building a relationship with each and every family and to develop a sense of community by organizing events and opportunities to get the families together. Then everyone will find ways to support a child with challenging behavior, her family, and the teachers. This is not to say that parents will stop being concerned about their child's safety or the influence a child with challenging behavior may have on theirs, but it is far more likely that they will understand your commitment to providing quality care for every child and will work with you rather than against you.

Open Communication Is Important

You and your staff will also discover that there is more than one way to communicate with families. What is most vital to remember is not to build walls. When you and your teachers know each family, you will have an idea of how best to communicate your concerns about the behavior of their child. Some families first need to hear what their child is doing well; others know that their child's behavior is difficult and want you to gently get to the point.

One thing you can be sure of is that no family wants to feel judged or blamed. Most of all, they want you to accept them and treat them with respect and understanding. Some families are more private than others, but try your best to get to know what is happening in their lives so that you can understand the child better. Everyone has a story and some stories are happier than others. Did they just move into the community or the country? Is this the first time their child is in a group situation? Have the parents recently separated? Is there a new baby in the family?

Meeting with the Family

When the teachers feel that a child's repeated problem behavior is interfering with the other children's ability to learn or threatening their safety, it's important to arrange a meeting to inform the family about the incidents and learn more about the child's behavior at home. Educators tend to blame the family, but they're not the enemy; they're your partners and you're all in this together. This is a difficult discussion to have, but it can be even more difficult if the teacher hasn't already made a significant effort to get to know this particular family. They want you and the teachers to be committed to their child, not to see your work as merely a job. They want to trust you, to know that you will do what you say you'll do, that you will keep their child safe, respect her, and make good things happen for her.

Who Should Attend a Meeting with the Family?

The teacher was present when the behavior occurred, and she should be building a relationship not only with the child but also with the family. She should therefore be the one to request the meeting and the one to meet with the family initially. Your presence may put extra pressure on the family and intimidate everyone, including the teacher. However, there may be times when you feel that your attendance at that meeting will emphasize its importance and the need for the family to take things seriously. Whether or not you join the teacher in meeting with a family or decide she should meet alone with them can be a difficult call, so be sure to discuss what is best for the child with your educator.

Whoever is making the request can see the family at pick-up time and let them know that there's a problem they would like to discuss at the family's convenience and that they will follow up with a phone call to make the arrangements. If the child ordinarily goes home with someone other than a parent or guardian, you or the teacher should phone the family and ask to arrange a meeting. Some parents may want to know all the details immediately, but you must resist the temptation to discuss the matter in front of the child or on the phone and instead emphasize the value of meeting when everyone can be there and will have time to talk. If possible, parents who are separated or divorced should both take part, so that everyone hears the same information and participates in the same discussion. If other family members such as grandparents play a big role in the child's life, including them can be helpful. The child needs everyone's support.

Planning the Meeting Together

Before the meeting, get together with the teacher to discuss how she plans to handle the situation. Because the message she is relaying to the family may be a difficult one for them to hear and accept, it's important for her to figure out specific ways to describe the incident. Saying the child is aggressive or easily frustrated doesn't tell the parents much—they can interpret these words in any way they choose—and a judgmental approach that associates their child with language they find objectionable will probably shut down any real communication.

The teacher will make a much stronger impression if she has incident reports and can give specific details about what happened: for example, that Carmen hit three children and kicked the teacher in the shins when it was time to clean up and that she kicked the teacher again when it was time to come inside after outdoor play. Using the incident reports to enumerate the times and days of the events, she should emphasize that this behavior occurs frequently and indicates that Carmen has difficulty during transitions. This description is much clearer and may well ring true with the family if she's behaving in a similar way with them. Advise the teacher to ask the family what they see at home, how they respond to the child's behavior, what responses are successful (or not), and how they can work together to make the home and school responses more consistent.

The Role of Implicit Bias and Culture in Teacher–Family Interactions

Before the teacher holds a meeting with the child's family, it is also essential to help her identify her own biases—explicit and implicit—that may make it difficult for her to have an open discussion with the family. For example, she may unconsciously react negatively to a parent who's overweight or a family with low income. Remind her that culture may be playing a role either in the behavior itself or in the way the teacher is perceiving the child and the family and that a behavior that's unacceptable at school may be acceptable at home.

Many teachers are not aware of how their cultural expectations of children's behavior may differ from the family's. In some cultures, children will show their interest in an activity by raising their voices and all talking at once, whereas at the school or center children may need to wait their turn, raise their hands, and speak one at a time. They may refuse to come to circle time because the teacher has phrased her implicit command as a question ("Carmen, won't you join us at circle?"), which in her culture means that you're offering her a choice. Discipline strategies also vary from culture to culture. In some cases, removing a child from the group is interpreted by the child as rejection. In cultures where discipline is handled by male family members and in cultures where spanking is the primary form of discipline, children might not take any guidance seriously, especially from women.

Whenever a cultural conflict between a family and you or your staff arises, it is important to listen carefully, be respectful, and understand their approach at the same time that you try to explain why things may be different in your program from the way they are in the child's home. This may be one of those situations where it is best for you to approach the family so that neither the teacher nor the family becomes defensive. If the family disagrees or simply disregards your views—which they may do without telling you because in their culture harmony is an important value and confrontation is considered rude—don't give up. They may be more receptive when they can see that their child's behavior is improving at the program and possibly even at home. (For more about cultural conflicts, see Chapters 5 and 7.)

If the family members speak limited English, ask them to bring an interpreter or allow you to find one. Do not ask an older sibling or other family member to interpret—this would put both the family member and the family in an awkward position and might turn the family's power structure upside down. If the family member who was interpreting felt that the topic was too personal or disagreed with what was being said, he might choose to convey something different in his translation.

Even when you and the family have cultural differences, you and your staff must continue to take your commitment to the child seriously and support her for the time she attends the program. It is still possible that you can make a difference.

How Should You Handle Disagreements with the Family?

Not all families are willing or able to accept what the teacher is telling them. Regardless of how well she presents the behavior incidents and the circumstances around them, they may not be ready to hear about their child's challenging behavior, and they may blame the teacher or another child, believe their child was provoked, or say she doesn't behave that way at home. They may also feel that the teacher doesn't recognize their efforts or understand their lives, or they may be afraid there's something wrong with their child. In addition, it's possible that they will blame and judge themselves, feel isolated, guilty, or depressed, and think they're bad parents. If they're upset and angry enough, they may even decide to look for another program.

Remind the teacher to listen to them carefully—if the parents feel heard, they may also feel more comfortable and receptive. The teacher may discover that there is a great deal of stress in their lives. Maybe they are afraid of being deported, the father has just lost his job, they're having trouble making ends meet, a family member is in prison, the child's grandmother recently passed away, or they are expecting another child and Carmen isn't happy about it.

If the child in question is an only child who doesn't spend much time with children outside the program, the family is probably telling you the truth when they say that they don't see a lot of challenging behavior at home. Or if both parents are studying or working full time or have two or three jobs, they may have little time to be with their children and may not even be aware of the problem. If an older child is in charge, he may not want to upset the parents; if there is a nanny, she may be afraid she'll be fired if she tells them she is encountering difficulties. However, in most cases it's likely that the behavior you and your teachers are seeing in the program is also happening at home. Families may not make the connection because the behavior may take a different form in a different context—for example, the child may scream and hit her mother when it's time to stop playing and come to dinner—but the family may not equate this with the problems she's having with transitions at the program.

If the child's behavior persists and the teacher is still feeling frustrated, this may be the time to hold another meeting where you join the teacher and the family in the conversation. The key to working successfully with all families, especially families of children with challenging behavior, is to keep the lines of communication open at all times.

What About Suggesting Families Seek Outside Help?

Some behaviors can lead you and your staff to believe that perhaps the child needs extra outside help and the family should consult a doctor. In this situation, you must be present when the information is conveyed. The issue is delicate, and the family may well say they don't need any assistance.

Your best hope of enlisting the family's support and cooperation is to be specific. Again using your incident reports, tell them exactly what the child is doing, why you and the educator feel it is necessary for them to seek external expertise, and that their family doctor or a specialist can make a diagnosis that will help everyone better understand the child's behavior and enable the staff to use preventive and responsive strategies that will work.

If the family is open to the idea and can see the benefits, your role may be to help them navigate this new territory. They should start by seeing their pediatrician or family physician and asking for a referral to the appropriate specialist if the doctor recommends it. In case they don't have a doctor or health insurance, be prepared with a list of options and some suggestions of how to follow up on your conversation. For example, you might find out about local community clinics, urgent care facilities, low-cost mental health clinics, and psychiatric emergency rooms. You can also tell them about organizations that can help them find resources and assistance, such as Partnership for Prescription Assistance and Needy Meds. It is irresponsible to tell any family, but especially families with limited income, families newly arrived in the community, or non-English speakers, that they need help and then expect them to figure out how to get it on their own. When you provide this support, you can also follow up with them, continue the conversation, and demonstrate that you and your teachers care about their child.

How Do You Work with the Families of the Other Children?

It is hard enough to work with trained, experienced staff when it comes to accepting the presence of a child with challenging behavior, but what do you say to families when their children are coming home with bruises or stories about a classmate who hurt them or their friend or upset their teacher? Families may threaten to withdraw their child from the school or center unless you switch him into a different classroom or expel the child with challenging behavior; and because they think that requiring a child to leave is the decision of the director or the principal, they may come first to you. Meanwhile, you have either decided on your own that you will not or cannot suspend or expel the child or know that you must follow state or district directives that prohibit this action.

Parents want their communication with you and the teachers to be frequent, open, honest, and nonjudgmental. Even if you can't do as they ask, they want to feel recognized and respected and to be able to trust you, and they need to believe that you and the educators have the skills and commitment to keep every child safe. If you and your staff are working together and have both preventive and responsive strategies in place, you can confidently let the families know in general terms that you're aware of the problem and explain that you are working with all the children to develop their social and emotional skills, including empathy, problem solving, and conflict resolution, and that you have (for example) already hired an additional person to work with the child and support the teachers.

This is certainly not the only time their child will encounter another child who threatens his sense of safety and well-being. It is important to emphasize what their child can learn from the experience: to understand that some children have a harder time expressing their feelings or getting along with others and to discover that even when children act in aggressive or frightening ways, they often have positive attributes as well.

Although most families will know who the child is, it is important to be as general as you can, remembering that confidentiality is important. So as much as you might want to tell other families that the child with challenging behavior was physically or sexually abused as a toddler, you cannot mention these facts. You may not even be able to confirm who she is or what she has done, but of course the families usually know—their own child has told them everything in great detail. Your emphasis must be on helping the parents of the other children understand that behavior is a form of communication and you are working with the teachers to figure out the message and teach the child in question more appropriate ways to meet her needs.

Is There a Better Alternative to Your Program?

There is no doubt that children need a stable environment where they can build supportive relationships and learn. But the sad reality is that even if your program has an excellent ratio and terrific teachers and you have been using proven preventive strategies and interventions and you've addressed potential cultural conflicts and implicit bias with your staff, it still may not be the best place for every child. In this situation, the family may recognize that there may be a better placement for the child, one that truly meets the child's (and the family's) needs, and you can help them find it. Once the family is in agreement, you need to work together to research possible alternatives with smaller groups, better ratios, and more access to support staff and resources, such as occupational therapists, language therapists, special education teachers, and behavioral consultants, who would be better equipped to meet their child's needs. Check waiting times, suggest that the family visit the new center or school and transition their child gradually so that he doesn't feel as though he has been rejected, and assure them that their child is welcome to stay until there is a place for him at another school or service. As you and your staff increasingly improve at addressing challenging behavior and trauma, it's possible that you may never need to make such a suggestion to a family again. (See also Chapter 4.)

Working with the family whose child's behavior is threatening the safety and well-being of your staff and the other children or disrupting activities throughout the day is never easy. Remember that you all have the same goal: to find ways together to teach their child the skills he needs to reach his potential.

For Further Learning

Koralek, D., K. Nemeth, & K. Ramsey. 2019. *Families & Educators Together: Building Great Relationships that Support Young Children.* Washington, DC: NAEYC.

CHAPTER ELEVEN
Helping Teachers Respond Effectively to Challenging Behavior

After Andrew and Carmen went to kindergarten, we continued searching for effective responses to disruptive and aggressive behavior. A few years later Kareem arrived, and during the orientation period for new children and families, the teachers called me for help. As soon as I entered the room, I realized that Kareem was truly out of control. I quickly reviewed all the strategies we'd been working on. He was surprised when I decided to sit at his feet, but after a moment he sat down beside me and allowed me to play with him and his trucks. I told him my name, he told me his, and a conversation about trucks followed. Within a few minutes another child approached and asked if he could play, too. I asked Kareem if it was all right, and he said "Sure" with a big smile. *Well done*, I thought as I saw the other children resume their play and the parents on the sidelines relax. I started to move away, but Kareem's expression darkened abruptly and he grabbed the big truck. I made up my mind to stay nearby for the remainder of the orientation, and Kareem did just fine.

Because your teachers are human—and possibly desperate—they may be looking for a quick fix for challenging behavior. But as you may have gathered by now, this chapter comes toward the end of this book because there is no quick fix, no single strategy or technique that will work for every child and every teacher in every situation. Challenging behavior doesn't come out of nowhere, and no strategy works in a vacuum. But all of the information in the previous chapters can help, and we will refer to those here from time to time.

It is not unusual for educators to feel overwhelmed and frustrated by a child with challenging behavior. It's unlikely that aggressive, disruptive behavior was a major focus of their education or training. Even if the topic came up, reading about it is far different from facing it in person, where one child seems capable not only of making it impossible to finish an activity but also of endangering himself, the other children, and the teacher. And the worst part is that most teachers don't know what to do about it. They may have learned, used, and believed in some of the punitive strategies that follow, but these strategies usually aren't very effective and certainly don't teach the children what they need to know to behave more appropriately.

Why Punishment Isn't Effective

There is no doubt that punishment will stop challenging behavior most of the time, and many teachers who are already overwhelmed feel that they don't have the time or ability to respond in any other way. We all tend to discipline the way we were disciplined. But punitive, aversive consequences—like time-out or sending a child to your office—won't actually change inappropriate behavior or teach the child better ways to behave.

Time-Out

Time-out is an automatic choice for many teachers who don't believe it's a punishment, and for that reason it's a good subject for discussion with your staff. You can help them to examine what time-out really means and how it might negatively impact a child's sense of self. For example, it can

> Damage the relationship between adult and child and undermine trust

> Make children angry and resentful and even inspire aggression

> Normalize the use of power as a means of control

> Create loneliness, sadness, fear, and insecurity (Readdick & Chapman 2000)

> Label a child as bad and unwanted, which is an especially harsh punishment for a child whose culture values belonging to the group or for a child who's experienced trauma

Some teachers will claim that they use time-away, a variant of time-out where the educator attempts to direct the child to another activity by making a suggestion like "Kareem, if you're having a problem playing in the dramatic play area, maybe you should look at a book." Usually this suggestion does not include the teacher moving with the child. While the teacher's tone of voice and body language can make the suggestion more or less punitive, both time-out and time-away require the child to move from one area to another, and it's unlikely that a child who is generally noncompliant and who has just spit on another child will agree to leave his peers and read a book. What will the teacher do when the child refuses? Will she spend 15 minutes trying to convince him? Will she yell at him? Or carry him to the book corner? Or will she just not follow through? What will the rest of the children conclude from witnessing such a struggle? Remind the teachers that saving face is just as important to the child as it is to the teacher.

It's also important to help teachers recognize that even when time-out or time-away stops the child from spitting, his challenging behavior may reappear at any time because he still doesn't know any other way to get what he needs or wants. A response to a child's challenging behavior that doesn't change the behavior or teach the child an appropriate way to express his feelings or meet his needs is not effective for the child, the other children, or the teacher.

Sending a Child to the Office

Whether you're the principal of a school or the director of a child care center, you are the safety net for your teachers. But this doesn't mean that sending you a disruptive, angry, or frustrated child is a good solution to a teacher's problem. This action disempowers the teacher and gives the child the message that she can't handle him, doesn't like him, or worse, doesn't care about him. He may also feel embarrassed and rejected—just as he does when a teacher puts him in time-out—and what will she do when he refuses to leave the room?

To be realistic, however, it is important for you to recognize that some situations really are overwhelming, and some educators, especially those with little experience or training, do not know what else to do. With their commitment, your support, and the appropriate professional development, they can learn how to respond successfully to children with challenging behavior. But in the meantime, while they're learning to handle the situation, bringing or sending the child to spend time with you may be the best option, provided the teacher tells you he's coming and fills you in on what happened. If you have a relationship with the child, you can go to the classroom to get him.

You might be tempted to call the family to come pick up the child, but the truth is that family members are unlikely to understand the gravity of the situation. What happens in the school or center should be dealt with there, and it is usually best for you or the teacher to immediately address such problems one-on-one with the child in a private space on the premises. When the child is calm, ask open-ended questions that can help him to understand what he did, the effect it had upon others, and what he thinks he could have done instead (Wright, n.d.).

> As soon as he arrived in the morning, Andrew quietly checked out what was happening. Then he picked up an empty plastic bucket and flung it across the room. It hit the window, and glass shattered everywhere. The other children immediately looked around for an adult. We told them not to move so that they wouldn't get hurt and started to assess and clean up the damage.
>
> Although I didn't believe in having the teachers send children to my office, I was so angry at the thought of what could have happened that I broke my rule and took Andrew with me. I sat him down in my office and told him why I was angry. Then I called his father, told him what had happened, and asked him to come pick up his son. When he walked in the door, the first thing his father said was, "I left early to see you. Let's go get an ice cream."
>
> I couldn't believe my ears. Needless to say, I learned my lesson: What happens at the center should be dealt with at the center!

Helping Your Staff Find Effective Alternatives

It isn't easy to change teachers' attitudes about the effectiveness of their responses to challenging behavior. They often feel they've tried everything, and the only thing that works is removing the child from the activity, the group, or the classroom. Help them to understand that punishing one child has a negative impact on all the children and creates a very negative classroom culture. It's up to you to help them feel comfortable with alternatives to punishment—which, incidentally, will be more effective.

What Your Teachers Need to Know

What guidance can you give to your teachers about the numerous strategies that claim to address challenging behavior? First of all, talk with them about what they feel a strategy should accomplish, and ask if they think that their own responses in actual situations are meeting those criteria. Point out that no strategy, no matter how effective it may be, will work unless teachers

> Cultivate a strong, positive relationship with every child in their group

> Create an inclusive, prosocial climate and ensure that the program is developmentally appropriate and individualized so that every child can succeed (see Chapter 6)

> Stay in control of their own emotions and know how to deal with an amygdala hijack

> Address the child's behavior, not the child herself

> Are flexible and patient, but maintain high expectations

> Look for the message the child is communicating with her behavior, as well as the skills she requires to meet her needs appropriately

> Start fresh every day, even if yesterday was a disaster (Kaiser & Rasminsky 2017)

WHAT A STRATEGY SHOULD ACCOMPLISH

In *FLIP IT!* Rachel Sperry (2011, 16) tells us that a strategy should

> "Help to strengthen the teacher's relationship with the child."

> "Address the root cause or the feelings behind the behavior."

> "Help the child learn how to [recognize and] control his/her emotions."

> "Help the child to become a problem-solver."

> "Help make long-term changes in the child's behavior."

Know Your Teachers

Every teacher is different. For some, keeping control of the classroom through rules and consequences is important, while others are happier providing fewer rules and offering children more choices (see Chapter 3). These views come from the teacher's own personality, experience, culture, and values, and they influence how he sees his role when challenging behavior occurs. It's important to work with each educator to find strategies that will support the child but won't compromise his beliefs. Most will be comfortable using natural and logical consequences and several other possibilities discussed in this chapter. When teachers have several strategies at their command, they can select the one that best fits the child and the circumstances—and if that approach doesn't work, they will have another to try.

Inform Yourself

Being well informed is another of a leader's basic responsibilities. You probably know more than your teachers about most things to do with early childhood education, and in particular you should know more about effective ways to address challenging behavior. This obliges you to keep your eyes and ears open for new ideas and research—to read books and journals and follow social media sites and blogs, always checking to make sure that your sources are reliable.

Your role also dictates that you belong to professional and community organizations and go to conferences and workshops, especially those that your teachers are attending. When they return to school excited about new theories and techniques, you have to know what they're talking about and be ready to help them put their ideas into practice.

In addition, it's essential for you to network with other administrators on a regular basis. You'll get to know about the resources in your area, and as a group, you may be able to afford to bring in professional development providers. (See Chapter 8 for more about professional development.)

Set a Positive Tone

Helping your teachers to maintain a positive attitude (and maintaining one yourself) is another key to supporting them. There is so much anger and frustration in dealing with challenging behavior day after day that teachers need tools to keep themselves going, give themselves a push, and prevent secondary traumatic stress, a condition that can be brought on by helping children and families exposed to trauma (Erdman & Colker with Winter 2020). (See Chapter 13.) Urge your teachers to get this boost by practicing self-reflection, journaling, or mindfulness (see Chapter 5) and by participating in regular staff meetings where they can speak freely and honestly and get input from you and their colleagues or look back and see that the child with challenging behavior really is making progress. All of this will enable your educators to pinpoint exactly which skills and professional development they need. (See Chapter 8.)

To keep everyone's mood up, it helps to plan some wacky days, like pajama or backwards day. Arrange some social gatherings or retreats where people can just relax, have a good time, and enjoy being together.

The Importance of Responding to Early Signs of Challenging Behavior

As we've said, challenging behavior doesn't come out of nowhere. Most teachers can tell as soon as a child arrives in the morning that he is likely to have a difficult day, but they haven't really thought about *how* they know this. Indeed, teachers can see challenging behavior in its embryonic form when they observe signs of anxiety, which they can recognize when they know a child well. Encourage them to notice and record how each child looks when he's feeling good about himself, interacting comfortably with his peers, and doing something he enjoys. At the same time, they should document just how the child looks when his expression or behavior changes, indicating that he's anxious and taking his first steps toward challenging behavior.

Help your teachers to look for these typical signs of anxiety:

> Physiology: tears, frequent urination, clenched teeth, blushing, pallor, rigidity, rapid breathing, sweating, fidgeting, squeaky voice

> Behavior: downcast eyes; withdrawing; twirling hair; sucking thumb, fingers, hair, or clothes; hoarding; clinging; biting fingernails; whining; rocking; being noisy or quiet; screaming; masturbating; smirking; giggling; crying (Butchard & Spencler 2011)

When a child's characteristic red flags appear, that is the moment for the teacher to support him in one or more of these ways:

> Approach and offer to sit with him for a while.

> Ask open-ended questions ("How was your morning?," "What did you have for breakfast?").

> Encourage him to think about what he's feeling ("Do you need a hug?").

> Validate and paraphrase whatever he says and show that she understands both his words and the message behind them ("I know it's hard when your friends start building a tower without you. Would you like me to help you join them?").

> Reframe a situation positively if that can be done honestly.

> Consider trying to match the child's voice pattern, which his anxiety may make unusually fast or slow, loud or soft. By gradually relaxing her own voice, a teacher can lead the child into speaking more normally and feeling more at ease, therefore less likely to ramp up his behavior. (Butchard & Spencler 2011)

Let your teachers know that you're aware of how task intensive mornings are and how difficult and time consuming this process of connecting with the child early on can be, but emphasize how incredibly important it is for the child. (See more about managing mornings on page 60 in Chapter 6.)

Several Effective Strategies

If a child's behavior continues to escalate, the teacher may need a different approach. And if punishment isn't the answer, what is? There are numerous options, but it's important to explore those that are research based and that have been proven effective first. Several possibilities follow in no particular order. Help your teachers to figure out which strategy relates best to the function of the behavior (see Chapter 12), their relationship with the child, and their own comfort level.

Provide Positive Guidance

As we said in Chapter 6, educators tend to tell children what not to do—"No hitting," "Stop running"—but such a command doesn't give enough guidance. Indeed, it is far more effective to calmly say "Carmen, please keep your hands to yourself" or "Kareem, please walk." Remind your teachers to speak from a reasonable distance—not to shout across the room—and to use the child's name to be sure they have her attention before they tell her what to do.

Offer a Choice

Offering a child a choice when he's behaving inappropriately is empowering for the child and is also an effective way to derail him from his usual track and switch him to a more rational one. When the teacher asks him to make a decision and choose between two possibilities, he has to think—so instead of allowing his feelings and his amygdala to run the show, his prefrontal cortex goes to work just the way it does when the teacher thinks about an arithmetic problem to stop her own amygdala hijack. (See page 37.)

This idea is far from new, and your teachers may say that they've tried it and it doesn't work. This gives you an opportunity to go into the classroom and see for yourself what the teacher is doing and how she is doing it. To repeat, to attract the child's attention, she should begin by using his name—"Kareem, you have a choice"—and then present the two options, neither of which should be punitive—"You can sit beside me, or next to Luisa." The child gains some time to pull himself together as he thinks over his choices. The teacher's tone of voice and body language are critical here. She should remain calm and relaxed so that the situation doesn't turn into a power struggle.

Because the child's actions will tell the teacher what he has decided to do, she needn't repeat the choices. If he hasn't made a choice after several minutes, she can offer a related choice: "Kareem, you can sit on my right side, or on my left side," using gestures to show what she means. She shouldn't repeat the choices or say, "You did this yesterday. I know you can do it." But she can ask, "Would you like some help making a choice, or do you want me to choose for you?" If he chooses but then changes his mind, that is perfectly all right, and the teacher should accept his decision graciously.

Surprise the Child

Children who have been using their behavior as a successful way to meet their needs also know how their families and teachers will respond to it. Sometimes the best way to stop children's challenging behavior is to react in a manner that surprises them instead of telling them what to do. Such a move, which WEVAS (Working Effectively with Violent and Aggressive States; Butchard & Spencler 2011) calls the "interrupt" and which worked with Kareem in the vignette at the beginning of this chapter, also allows the child to save face. When the teacher tells Treyvon to stop climbing on the shelf or reminds him that his feet should stay on the floor, chances are he will climb higher because that is exactly what he expected to hear. But if she asks for his help or takes out a game or an activity that he enjoys such as building with magnetic shapes, he's likely to stop climbing and join her. Then she'll have an opportunity to calmly say that climbing on the shelf is dangerous. She should avoid asking why he's climbing. The context of the incident should be self-explanatory: he likely wants her attention or an object that is out of reach, or he just loves climbing. She will have prevented a win-lose situation, avoided drawing attention to his behavior, and most important of all, kept him from feeling humiliated.

Natural and Logical Consequences

Remind your teachers that natural and logical consequences are teaching tools—and if the child is going to learn anything from them, they must be related to his behavior (Dreikurs with Soltz 1964).

Natural consequences are those that happen all by themselves in a course of events. If it's raining and Carmen won't put on her boots, her shoes and socks will get wet and she will be uncomfortable; if Ethan talks to his neighbor while the teacher is explaining what to do, he won't be able to follow the instructions. If they're having fun, they may not care at the time, but they will eventually. Sometimes however, teachers may make matters clearer by creating logical consequences instead. When Kareem deliberately pours water on the floor at snack time, the consequence can be that he gets a towel and helps the teacher clean it up. In either case, the child discovers that he has control over his life as well as responsibility for what he does. He is learning to make decisions and a better way to show his feelings.

On the other hand, when the consequences don't relate to the child's behavior, they are not really consequences but a form of punishment. Teachers should take care not to make logical consequences disrespectful or punitive. For example, when Kareem pours water on the floor, the teacher should not say that he won't get any more water or that he needs to sit by himself; or when Ethan doesn't listen to the directions, the teacher should not deprive him of his recess time. This is more likely to happen when a teacher uses the consequences to express her own anger. Your teachers should also consider the possible unintended results of a consequence, such as letting a child avoid an activity he struggles with or doesn't like (see pages 12 and 118 in Chapters 2 and 12, respectively).

As a group, you and your staff might also explore the difference between punishment and natural and logical consequences. Make the discussion fun by creating a series of cards with specific behaviors that the teachers are seeing and ask them to come up with some natural or logical consequences. Having a range of choices will enable them to select one that is both helpful and appropriate for the circumstances (Curwin, Mendler, & Mendler 2008). As a consequence for hitting, they may suggest making sure the other child is okay, getting ice to put on the bruise, or letting the child know it's all right to be angry but it's not okay to hit. Then teacher and child can talk about how he can tell his peer that he wants to play with the cash register.

Explain to your teachers that requiring a child to apologize doesn't help him to understand what he did and may lead him to believe that it's okay to hurt another child or take her toy or throw things across the room as long as he says he's sorry.

One useful consequence is a private meeting with the teacher (Smith 2004), which allows both teacher and child to calm down, save face, and escape an unpleasant confrontation. This is totally different from time-out or time-away, when the teacher is asking the child, probably with a stern voice or expression, to do something that's unrelated to his behavior. Instead she's accompanying the child and remaining open to his needs, saying, "Let's talk about this," finding a quiet space for them to sit down together, and turning the situation into a learning opportunity that strengthens her relationship with the child. For example, if the teacher asks him, "When you hit Luisa, what were you trying to tell her?" his response will probably be "I was playing with the truck," which gives her the opening to ask "What else could you have done?"

Collaborative and Proactive Solutions

Collaborative and Proactive Solutions (CPS, previously known as Collaborative Problem Solving) is a strategy developed by Dr. Ross Greene, author of *The Explosive Child*, *Lost at School*, and *Lost and Found*. It begins with the understanding that children behave the way they do for a reason, and when they lack the skills to meet the expectations placed on them, challenging behavior may well be the outcome. CPS is composed of three main steps, all of which should occur in calm, one-on-one conversations between the teacher and the child in order to

› Gather information to understand the child's perspective

› Define the problem from the adult's point of view

› Collaborate to find a solution that recognizes both points of view

The idea is for the child and the adult to solve their problem collaboratively, without conflict or punishment, by identifying and remediating missing skills (Lives in the Balance, n.d. a). Clearly this strategy will be more successful if the educator is already actively working to build »ationship with the child and teaching social and emotional skills.

Implementing CPS may be difficult for teachers who need to be in control or who believe they should be in control. Help them to understand the value of compromise and of picking their battles, even with very young children. For example, a 26-month-old might really need his cuddly (comfort object) with him at all times. For a teacher, this seems impractical because the cuddly can easily get damaged or lost. What compromise can they reach? Perhaps during times when it might get damaged, they can wrap the cuddly in a towel; and when it could be misplaced or hinder the child from completing a task, the child and teacher could select a special safe spot to stow it. This solution not only avoids a meltdown but also helps develop problem-solving skills and enables the child to believe that the teacher understands and cares about him.

Planned Ignoring

Every child—every human being—needs attention, and some of us need more attention than others. Some children have learned that the best way to get attention is to engage in inappropriate behavior. Remind your teachers that a child's need for attention is very real—the problem is the way he seeks that attention (see Chapter 12). One way to change this scenario is to use planned ignoring, meaning that the teacher ignores the inappropriate behavior if she knows it won't endanger anyone. This means not reacting to it, not providing any reinforcement, not making eye contact or talking with the child. The teacher's failure to respond may elicit an extinction burst—that is, the child's behavior may escalate—but she should continue to ignore it. Needless to say, she must respond to behavior that's potentially or actually dangerous.

For this approach to work, the teacher must provide attention when the child behaves appropriately and even encourage him when he comes up with a close approximation of the desired behavior. Teachers frequently say that when they provide positive verbal reinforcement to a child with challenging behavior, he responds by acting out. Help them to recognize that this response indicates that the child lacks self-confidence and is uncomfortable because positive recognition of his behavior is so unusual. In this situation it's important to begin slowly with very gentle, specific encouragement that recognizes the child's effort or persistence. It is absolutely crucial to choose something that the child can tolerate easily, perhaps just a smile, a secret signal, or a thumbs up. Teachers should be aiming to help him become comfortable with any meaningful form of positive reinforcement, but they have to remember that getting there must be a gradual process and will take time. For example, if Treyvon has been throwing his coat into the middle of the classroom but instead throws it into the cubby area, the teacher can recognize this as a first step and say "Well done. Your coat is in the room where it belongs. Next step—let's find the right hook." (A warning: When using this strategy, teachers must be very careful not to be sarcastic.)

The Penny-Transfer Technique

If one of your teachers seems to have an especially hard time developing a positive attitude toward the children and her responsibilities, the penny-transfer technique can encourage her to find those rewarding moments, recognize a child's positive contribution to the day, develop a positive classroom culture, and enhance her own enjoyment and job satisfaction. Focusing this technique on a particular child with challenging behavior may make it easier for her to respond in a calmer, more effective manner.

The technique asks her to start the day with five pennies in her right-hand pocket and transfer one penny to her left-hand pocket every time she finds a way to engage positively with the child in question. The goal is to empty the right-hand pocket by the day's end. If she notices any progress, she can up the ante and use 10 or 15 more pennies. In time, she should see an improvement in the child's behavior and in her own relationship with him and the other children.

When a Child Loses Control

A child who is out of control is very frightening to everyone—to the child's classmates as well as the teacher herself. If a teacher is truly desperate and afraid that a child will hurt himself or others, the teacher may consider using a form of restraint, but restraint is never an option unless she has been trained and has permission to use it as part of a behavior plan developed by a team that includes the family and a mental health professional.

Restraint is intrusive, punitive, and traumatic and can actually injure the child or the teacher. A child who has lost control is probably being asked to do something he doesn't have the skills to do (Lives in the Balance, n.d. b) and restraint won't help solve the underlying problems or prevent the behavior in the future. Instead, all staff should be trained to use nonviolent crisis intervention techniques, which the Individuals with Disabilities Education Act requires for children with disabilities.

Make a Clear Plan

There should be a clear plan in place to deal with a situation when a child has lost control and is engaging in a tantrum, yelling, throwing things across the room, attacking another child, or destroying property.

Keep the Children Safe

How can your teachers let you know when they need your help? Create a code such as "Code Blue" that in just two words tells you to drop everything and head for the classroom. Some rooms may connect to your office by intercom, or the teacher can send a responsible child to say she needs your help. Although centers and schools often prohibit cell phones in the classroom, in an emergency they can be extremely useful, so it might be wise to make an exception and put your office number on speed dial on every teacher's cell.

To keep the other children safe, the director or principal should take them out of the room, a maneuver that you and your teachers must organize in advance. This action will also remove the audience, who may be embarrassing the child and who may escalate the challenging behavior simply by watching. Take a walk around the center or school to figure out where you and a group of children can settle for however long it takes for the child to calm down. (The first few times that you and the teacher use this technique, it may take half an hour or more.) Can you go to the gym, the cafeteria, the library, another classroom, the play yard? To maintain the required ratio, other staff members should also be prepared to step in.

Who Stays with the Child?

It is important for the teacher to remain with the child and help him calm down because that is what will strengthen their relationship. (Remember, if the director or principal takes over, it disempowers the teacher in the mind of both the child and the teacher herself.) Once she is alone with the child, the teacher can concentrate on working with him. If there are two teachers in the classroom, the one with the better relationship with the child should remain; the other can exit with you and the other children. Your teachers usually know which role to take, but this information should be part of the plan.

Remind your teachers that when a child truly loses control it is not a teachable moment. His feelings, not his reason, are in charge of his behavior, and talking to him may make things worse. Before he can hear a single word a teacher says, he must regain control of his emotions.

In these circumstances, your most important task is to help your teachers remember to stay cool, calm, and collected so that they can think clearly, problem solve, and focus on deescalating the child's behavior. Staying cool isn't easy for any teacher, and it's especially hard when the child's behavior has provoked her and both she and the child are experiencing an amygdala hijack (see page 37). But this is what she must do if she is going to help him calm down.

Deescalating Challenging Behavior

The teacher should stay where the child can see and hear her, and she can let him know she's there in case he needs her. But if she can't talk to him, what should she do? How can she communicate with him? By using her body. This means carefully avoiding any posture that will threaten him, such as standing with her hands on her hips or allowing anger to show in her face. Instead she must seem open and relaxed and stay involved with him in a neutral way, adjusting slowly and deliberately to his behavior as it shifts. No matter what he says or does, she must not take it personally. To help her maintain this state of mind, she might use breathing and self-talk, imagine that she's somewhere pleasant, or simply concentrate on the bottoms of her feet.

Making sure that both child and teacher feel safe is imperative. WEVAS (Butchard & Spencler 2011) points out that the child will probably need more space than usual. It's also useful to teach your staff the centered L-stance (see the figure below), where the teacher stands sideways rather than facing the child. With her shoulder at right angles to the shoulders of the child, forming an L, she seems less intimidating. Because eye contact can inflame the situation, she should look over the child's shoulder or at his midsection and only make eye contact when he stops to take a breath or actually tries to calm himself down. This eye contact should give the message to the child that he is okay and that the teacher will help him to regain control.

The safest tactic is to let the child run out of steam. Because every child needs to breathe once in a while, the behavior will stop for a few seconds whether intentionally or not, and then the child will want to connect with the teacher. Once again, this is where body language and facial expression are important. The teacher can use eye contact to say "I'm here, I care" if the child is comfortable with it. But if he is still in challenging behavior mode and his tantrum continues (remember, it was just a breath), she just needs to be there and not make eye contact. Gradually he will begin to calm down and feel better, but she must keep her distance and judge whether he's ready to talk, reserving real eye contact as a reward for calmer behavior. If it seems to increase the behavior, she should look away and wait a little longer.

Once the child is calm, the teacher can begin to talk to him and acknowledge his feelings, but she must remember to choose her words carefully. Saying "we" instead of "you," "can" instead of "should," and "and" instead of "but" will prevent him from feeling threatened or shamed. For example, "I know you were very frustrated and that made you angry. Let's work together to find some ways to help deal with frustration." Or if he trashed the room, "Let's clean this up and put everything back where it belongs."

The goal is to provide the support the child needs to return to the group knowing that the teacher cares about him. A little while later she can help this process along with a private conversation about his feelings, what led to this event, and how they can handle things the next time around.

Educators are always looking for ways to respond to a child's challenging behavior. Your support and leadership skills are key here. It is not enough just to stop the behavior. Teachers must aim to change the behavior by providing children with the skills they need in order to be able to meet their needs appropriately.

For Further Learning

Books

Bailey, B.A. 2015. *Conscious Discipline: Building Resilient Classrooms* (expanded and updated). Oviedo, FL: Loving Guidance.

Dunlap, G. 2016. *Prevent-Teach-Reinforce for Families: A Model of Individualized Positive Behavior Support for Home and Community.* Baltimore, MD: Brookes.

Dunlap, G., & P. Strain. 2013. *Prevent-Teach-Reinforce for Young Children: The Early Childhood Model of Individualized Positive Behavior Support.* Baltimore, MD: Brookes.

Kaiser, B., & J.S. Rasminsky. 2017. *Challenging Behavior in Young Children: Understanding, Preventing, and Responding Effectively.* 4th ed. Columbus, OH: Pearson Education.

Periodicals

Young Children: NAEYC.org/resources/pubs/yc

Exchange: www.childcareexchange.com/catalog/magazine

Web Resources

ASCD: www.ascd.org

ContinuED: www.continued.com/early-childhood-education

Education Week: www.edweek.org/ew/index.html

Edutopia: www.edutopia.org

Hechinger Report: www.hechingerreport.org

National Center for Pyramid Model Innovations (NCPMI): https://challengingbehavior.cbcs.usf.edu

WEVAS: www.wevas.ca

CHAPTER TWELVE

Functional Assessment and Positive Behavior Support

Soon it became clear that there was a pattern to Kareem's behavior, so we decided to observe and record the times when he lost control. Because the teachers felt that they weren't often in the right place at the right time to capture the triggers or consequences of his challenging behaviors, I decided to observe him, too. When we looked at the data we'd collected, we realized that he behaved differently with each educator and that each teacher responded differently as well. We also saw that free play and noisy activities such as cleanup triggered his inappropriate behavior.

Kareem's actions seemed related to the level of stimulation in the room. When things became noisy and less structured, he screamed and threw things on the floor—except when he was with Carol. During free play she stayed beside him and managed to prevent meltdowns by explaining the choices, giving him specific tasks, and supporting his efforts to join in play with his peers. This discovery helped us to identify ways to prevent his challenging behavior as well as the skills we needed to teach him.

Schools and centers across the country use positive behavior support (PBS) as a universal, whole-school approach to create a positive school climate and prevent challenging behavior (Samuels 2013). PBS is a tiered strategy, meaning that it recognizes that different children have different levels of need for support and intervention. In order to help the 1 to 7 percent of those who require a more intensive, individualized approach, PBS is often paired with a technique called functional assessment or functional analysis (FA) or functional behavioral assessment (FBA). Developed by behavioral psychologists, FA enables educators to observe a child more closely and collect data that illuminates why the challenging behavior is occurring at a particular time in a particular place. With this information, it becomes possible to create an individual positive behavior support plan for the child.

The most important idea behind both strategies is that challenging behavior is a child's solution to a problem, and this behavior enables her to fulfill her needs. With the help of careful observation and the behavior incident reports you and your teachers have collected, FA allows teachers to figure out the purpose or function of the behavior as well as the events that trigger and maintain it.

With this information, they can create a behavior support plan that will empower them to teach the child more acceptable ways to get what she needs. Although an FA and behavior support plan are similar to an Individualized Education Program (IEP), their use is not limited to children with disabilities, but like an IEP they may require parental permission and are always most effective when families are engaged in the process.

If you feel that an FA and behavior support plan would be useful for a particular child, you have a few options. You and your staff can conduct the FA yourselves and build a behavior support plan together with the child's family. If a psychologist or social worker is already working with the child, he may be willing to become part of your team and observe and record the child's behavior as well. Or you could call in an outside expert from your school board or one of the many agencies that deal with children's mental health, your local resource and referral agency, the department of early learning in your area, or your school board (see Chapter 9).

How Does Functional Assessment Work?

As we noted in Chapter 2, FA postulates that there are three possible functions or purposes for a challenging behavior (O'Neill et al. 2015):

> To obtain an object or attention

> To avoid a person or task

> To change the level of stimulation (Karsh et al. 1995)

But discovering which of these possible functions applies in a particular child's situation is a complex affair involving data. It usually takes a team that includes you as the leader, the family, and anyone else who works with the child, including your teachers and teaching assistants, an after-school teacher, a psychologist, or a social worker, plus a lot of observation, interviews, and discussion (Fox & Duda, n.d.).

To determine the function or purpose of a child's challenging behavior, the team usually employs a method called an A-B-C analysis (Bijou, Peterson, & Ault 1968):

> *A* stands for antecedents, which occur just before the challenging behavior and act as a trigger for it—for example, a teacher's demands or requests, difficult tasks, or transitions (O'Neill et al. 2015).

> *B* stands for the child's specific challenging behavior, which must be described clearly enough for anyone on the team to recognize and measure its intensity and frequency without any subjective interpretation (O'Neill et al. 2015). It might be spitting, hitting the teacher, or running out of the room.

> *C* stands for consequences, which are the responses to the challenging behavior. They can be anything that follows it, including the reactions of the other children or the teacher, and because they usually reward the behavior, they are often called the *maintaining consequences*. Laughing, offering attention (either positive or negative), removing the child from an activity, even providing help can all be maintaining consequences.

It is important to keep in mind that completing an FA is key to identifying the rationale behind a child's behavior, so the more people who are trained and available to participate in this exercise, the clearer the picture will become.

Observing Children with Your Teachers

Information in the child's file and the behavior incident reports are a good place to start. But detailed observation of the child and the environment are the most important factors in identifying the function or purpose of challenging behavior.

Finding the time and ways to observe a child's challenging behavior as well as its antecedents and consequences is a daunting task even for teachers with degrees, who may or may not have learned to observe and record behavior properly. And because teaching young children is in itself so task intensive, your teachers may be concerned that they are already stretched to the limit. Nonetheless, they are probably the best possible observers because when an outside consultant enters the room, she will certainly alter the behavior of the child or the educator or both. (Of course, after a couple of visits, she won't be as obtrusive, and her knowledge of the whole process of FA and positive behavior support will help the team to work more smoothly and effectively.) You can do observations, too, and if you have been in the classroom regularly and often enough, your presence shouldn't affect anyone else's behavior.

What Do You and Your Team Need to Look For?

Before observing and recording the challenging behavior, the first step is to identify the exact **behaviors** that everyone is observing. Teachers often use general terms such as "defiant" or "aggressive," but this language isn't specific enough. It is much clearer to say that the child hits, kicks, screams, withdraws, or refuses to follow directions.

This precision will help the team to determine the **antecedents** of the behavior. Was the child busy playing when the teacher said it was time to clean up? Were the other children too close to him? Had the teacher been paying attention to his peers, but not to him? Was the room chaotic or too noisy, or were things moving too slowly at circle time?

Then it is important to observe and record the **consequences**. Did the other children laugh at him? Did the teacher reprimand him? Recording the consequences is difficult because it may require teachers to reflect on their own actions. For example, if a teacher rushes to a child who's pushing another child off a chair, she may be reinforcing the pushing—that is, if the child is pushing in order to get her attention.

You can help your teachers learn to observe by talking with them about ways they feel might work, such as keeping a pen and a small pad in their pocket to jot down a few notes right after the child calms down and before they forget what happened, or using their phone to record their impressions later. In this manner they can also capture valuable information about the behavior's trigger and response.

Your teachers should also be observing and recording times when the child is behaving appropriately so that they know what engages her, when and where she functions best, and who she enjoys being with. This information will be key when it comes time to build the positive behavior support plan. You'll find a blank A-B-C observation chart in Appendix 3.

Developing a Hypothesis

In addition, teachers should participate fully in the next phase of the FA procedure: using all the data they've collected so far to work with the team to develop a hypothesis—a possible explanation or theory about the behavior's function or purpose. The hypothesis will become the foundation for the team's behavior support plan (O'Neill et al. 2015). An example illustrating the entire process appears later in the chapter.

Creating a Behavior Support Plan

Once you've identified the behavior, the antecedents, and the consequences and figured out the behavior's function or purpose, your team is ready to construct a behavior support plan. You will need as many ideas and points of view as possible, so everyone on the team should participate, just as they did when they were working out the function of the behavior. The chart below is one illustration of how you might capture the ideas the team brainstorms before drafting the plan.

The child will resist efforts to change his behavior unless the replacement behavior is as efficient and effective as the problem behavior, so the plan should identify how the behavior can be prevented, the skills that the child needs to learn, and the responses that will encourage him to meet his needs appropriately. It's also important to keep the child's positive moments, his strengths, and his interests clearly in mind (Dunlap et al. 2006).

Child's name _____

Antecedent	Behavior	Maintaining Consequence
	Function	
Preventions	**Goals/Skills**	**New Responses**

Behavior Support Planning Chart. Adapted, by permission, from L. Fox and M.A. Duda, "Positive Behavior Support" (Technical Assistance Center on Social Emotional Intervention for Young Children). www.challengingbehavior.org

Prevention

Begin by thinking about specific ways to prevent the challenging behavior. This will entail finding and changing its antecedents in the classroom environment—in the physical space, activities, curriculum, routines, and even the teacher's own behavior, words, and expectations. It can be as simple as getting several more popular trucks and dolls, controlling numbers by placing fewer chairs at an activity table, and offering different ways for children to complete a task so that if they are uncomfortable finger painting, they can use a brush (or vice versa).

Replacement Behaviors

Next the team must decide which skills the child needs to learn and how they will help him replace his inappropriate behavior with appropriate behavior. Enabling the child to use an appropriate replacement behavior is the major goal. What can he do that serves the same purpose? What skills does he have to learn? This inevitably involves teaching (O'Neill et al. 2015). Perhaps the most common skills a child with challenging behavior needs to learn are how to ask for help and how to ask for a break, but the possibilities are many and various. He may require help with joining a group; with throwing and catching a ball; with managing anger or finding a quiet space or a way to reduce his anxiety when he feels overwhelmed. The team should identify the steps required for the child to learn the new skill and start by choosing a skill that's easy to learn, preferably one based on the child's strengths, so that he will quickly experience success.

> Kareem enjoyed playing with others but had trouble knowing how to join in if he didn't initiate the game himself. He would push his peers, bop them on their heads with toys, or yell to get their attention. The PBS team chose the goal of "Kareem will be able to join in play with his peers" and identified several ways for him to achieve it:
>
> › Stand nearby and observe the other children so that they might ask him to join them.
>
> › Offer a suggestion, like adding a truck to the fleet the others are playing with or showing them a new way to go down the slide.
>
> › Use specific words to ask if he can play, such as simply saying "Can I play with you?"

Responses to the Child's Behavior

The team must also select responses to use when the child behaves appropriately and when he behaves inappropriately. If the function of the behavior is to obtain attention, the team must remember that the child's need for attention is very real, and they must provide him with attention when he's acting appropriately (but not when he's acting inappropriately).

What form will this positive reinforcement take? Again, the teachers must focus on what the child enjoys and is good at and figure out how they will make extra time to talk and play with him. For example, if he likes puzzles, the teacher might decide to spend special time with him at the puzzle table. If he enjoys cooking or baking, she can create a cake-making project where he can act as the first assistant chef. Or she can plan to play with him and his beloved trucks or trains or bank time with him as Robert Pianta suggests (see page 51).

Working out ways to deal with the child's inappropriate behavior will probably be much more difficult because the team must respond without rewarding the behavior. In cases where the function of the behavior (such as pushing) is to obtain attention, they can plan to ignore it and choose a different response (such as talking first to the child being pushed) (see pages 108–109 in Chapter 11).

The team will need a different strategy when the child is trying to avoid something. Removing him from the situation would reward his challenging behavior, so the plan shouldn't offer that possibility. Instead it is crucial to focus on factors in the immediate environment so that you can figure out which ones trigger the behavior and how to change them. In such a situation the teacher must support the child so that he can take part. For example, Carmen has difficulty sitting and listening at story time and often pinches or hits the children nearby. To encourage her to participate, the teacher can make sure Carmen has worry beads or a stress ball to hold or invite Carmen to sit beside her, turn the pages of the book, or even choose the story. If Ethan feels he doesn't read as well as the other children and throws his book on the floor to save himself from embarrassment when it's his turn to read out loud, before the activity begins the teacher can ask him if he's comfortable reading out loud, and if he's uneasy, the teacher can assure him that they can practice together privately instead. These solutions may look like prevention, but of course they are preventive strategies and responses at the same time.

Last but not least, the plan should outline a method and timeline for evaluating progress.

What Happens Next?

Your teachers should be aware that as soon as they change their responses to the child's challenging behavior, it is likely to get worse. This phenomenon is known as an *extinction burst,* and it will pass. In addition, it may take up to six weeks for them to see the results of their efforts, especially if the challenging behavior has been part of the child's repertoire for a long time. Encourage the teachers to start by concentrating on small improvements that they may need your input to notice, such as that the child is using more positive behavior or that his outbursts are shorter, less frequent, or less violent.

Once again, an important reminder: start the FA and positive behavior support process well before your teachers are burned out and demanding that you ask the child to leave the program. Help them to remember that a child's challenging behavior is sending them a message: the task at hand is too difficult; the child doesn't understand the expectations; he needs their attention; the environment is too loud and chaotic. Of course, not all of the causes of challenging behavior are in the immediate environment, but it's helpful to look at the behavior in this way. If the teachers listen carefully to the child's message, they will be able to identify the skills he needs to learn, and ultimately they will become better teachers. Most of all, they need to let go of any negative feelings they have about the child's behavior and start fresh every day.

Using Functional Assessment and a Positive Behavior Support Plan: Ryan

The following is an example of how to create and implement a positive behavior support plan based on an FA.

Ryan's Background

You can gain a great deal of useful information by reading a child's file and interviewing his family and teachers.

Ryan is 4 years old. He has been at the Willow Tree Early Childhood Center for three months, and every week his behavior seems to be escalating and harder to control. His mother informed the center that from the age of 3 months he attended a family child care program where he didn't present any serious behavior problems, but when he outgrew it at 18 months, his parents moved him to an early childhood center near their home. After eight months at this center he was asked to leave because of his behavior. At this point his family had difficulty finding a child care place for him, so his grandmother took care of him. After they had a second child, the family moved and was able to enroll Ryan at Willow Tree.

Ryan is large for his age and has poorly developed large and fine motor skills. He can be very helpful and articulate, but he uses his words sparingly, and he often looks sullen and serious. He tries to make friends but doesn't seem to know how. His teacher, Anna, and other teachers have tried to build a relationship with him, but he rebuffs them and seems to prefer to maintain some distance.

The family has said that he has tantrums at home and throws things when his mom is nursing the baby or when he is asked to pick up after himself. He refuses to get dressed in the morning and gets upset over changes in routine.

Antecedents at the Program

The teachers have said that Ryan's behavior appears to be unpredictable and occurs throughout the day during structured and nonstructured activities, transitions, and frequently upon arrival. For the moment, no one knows what triggers his behavior.

Ryan's Behavior

Ryan pushes, kicks, and hurts his peers without warning and has thrown objects across the room and overturned furniture. As a result, the other children avoid him whenever possible.

The teachers have also noticed that Ryan enjoys doing puzzles and loves trains and trucks and sliding down the outside play structure. He seems to have one friend, Lucy, who also likes doing puzzles and loves the slide, although he often rejects her overtures to play.

Consequences of Ryan's Behavior

The teachers have been responding to Ryan's behavior in a variety of ways, including talking with him one-on-one, removing him from the group or activity, and sending him to the director's office. But regardless of how the teachers respond, no one has noticed any improvement in Ryan's behavior.

Conducting a Functional Assessment for Ryan

After consulting with Ryan's teachers and family, the director decides to call in a mental health consultant from the community resource center. The consultant suggests conducting an FA to determine the triggers or antecedents and maintaining consequences of Ryan's behavior so that they can create a positive behavior support plan together with the family. This will allow everyone to be on the same page and prevent as well as respond effectively to Ryan's aggressive behavior.

During several visits to the program, the consultant observes and records Ryan's behavior and the activities around it on an A-B-C chart. (There are completed versions of Ryan's A-B-C chart and a chart used to brainstorm ideas for his behavior support plan in Appendix 4 and Appendix 5, respectively.) She concludes that the function of Ryan's behavior is primarily to avoid activities or situations when he feels uncertain of his ability to succeed. He is especially uneasy with activities that involve large and fine motor skills. She bases her conclusions on his willingness to leave an activity that calls for these skills. For example, she witnesses an activity where the teacher has set up a relay race that requires the children to step through hoops laid on the floor. Seemingly as soon as Ryan realizes what the activity entails, he pushes the child beside him. His teacher asks him to keep his hands to himself, at which point he turns and kicks someone else. The teacher then tells him to sit on the bench and watch the activity. He does so without hesitation.

The consultant also makes a point of being at the center early in the morning to observe Ryan's behavior at arrival time. She notices that he stands by the door, looks around, then goes to an area, usually the block area, and knocks down whatever the other children are building.

She feels that, like most young children, Ryan wants attention and finds it easiest to obtain through his inappropriate behavior. For example, he sometimes pushes a child who is engaged in play with others and then walks away.

In addition, she notes that Ryan rarely smiles and appears to have a negative temperament that makes it hard for the educators to offer him support or attention except when he behaves inappropriately. He doesn't respond and shows little interest unless he starts the conversation.

Building a Behavior Support Plan for Ryan

The next step is to convene a meeting of everyone concerned with Ryan's care: his teachers, family (including his grandmother), the center's director, and the consultant. Together they will develop a behavior support plan that will help Ryan learn appropriate ways to meet his needs. It is important to note that his needs—the function of his behavior—are very real. The goal of a behavior support plan is to teach him how to meet his needs appropriately.

Identifying the Function

After examining the A-B-C chart and discussing Ryan's behavior at home and at school, the team comes to the conclusion that he most often acts out when trying to escape or avoid an activity that he doesn't want to do or feels he cannot do as well as his peers and is afraid of trying. Joining another child in play—building with blocks, drawing with markers, or dramatic play—is especially difficult for him. His first inclination is to knock over the blocks, grab others' drawings, or throw things on the floor.

Prevention

The group also discusses ways to prevent the behavior from occurring both at home and at the center. They select several possibilities. First, they acknowledge the importance of Ryan's knowing that they care. Everyone will make a conscientious effort to support his appropriate behavior and look for opportunities to connect with him. If the teachers or family recognize Ryan's anxiety or concern about his performance, they can offer help by modifying the task length, their expectations, and the materials while they introduce the activity. For example, during a large motor activity, instead of asking everyone to skip to the finish line, the teacher could give children the choice of jumping, crawling, hopping, or walking quickly. Or the teachers could make activities such as circle time a matter of choice so that Ryan can join when he is comfortable, leave when he needs to, and return if he wishes. They also decide to help him join in play with other children when he arrives in the morning, assigning his teacher, Anna, to stay nearby until he appears comfortable.

Next they discuss adding peer partnering activities so that Ryan will get peer support and perhaps make a friend. In addition, the family and teachers realize that noting and supporting any effort Ryan makes to try or work at an activity is far more important than praising the outcome. Finally, they decide to follow a least-preferred activity with a preferred one. Because Ryan doesn't like to participate in large motor activities, the teacher will tell him what the activity in the gym will be and she will be there to help him to try it out. If he decides he doesn't want to participate, he can help her to set it up instead. She will tell him that he can play with the trains when the activity finishes.

Goals

Everyone agrees that the long-term goal for Ryan is to be able to participate in all activities. The group identifies two short-term goals in order to track his progress:

1. When asked to participate in an activity that he feels is too difficult, Ryan will ask for help.

2. When Ryan does not want to participate, he will ask to leave the activity.

Responses

The response to or consequence of a child's behavior often supports the child's needs, whether the behavior itself is appropriate or inappropriate. Consistency is key, so the team discusses how the teachers and family will respond to both appropriate and inappropriate behavior. They note that they must be sure not to remove Ryan from an activity he finds difficult when he behaves inappropriately.

They identify the following possible responses to Ryan's challenging behavior:

> Offer assistance.

> Scaffold.

> Provide choices.

> Teach him to ask for help.

> Talk with him about appropriate ways to let others know what he needs.

> Identify his feelings with words.

When Ryan shows appropriate behavior, the adults will respond in these ways:

> Recognize Ryan's effort, persistence, and use of new strategies.

> Follow up with a favorite activity.

The Director or Principal's Role

The plan provides goals for Ryan, but establishing the plan is just the beginning. The hard part is implementing it. Now his teachers and family need to teach him the skills necessary to reach those goals. You can't tell parents how to parent unless they ask for your advice, but you are there to provide guidance and support to the teachers and help them to understand that the key to helping Ryan achieve the goals they've set is to build a strong relationship with him, no matter how hard or how often he pushes them away. Remind them that his behavior is expressing a need and their job is to teach him ways to meet that need appropriately. They should take some deep breaths and be sure not to take the behavior personally or to see it as a rejection, but rather as a cry for help.

In addition to letting him know that hitting, pinching, and other hurting behaviors are not okay, they must teach him appropriate ways to let others know what he needs and reassure him that they will help. When he asks for help, they must really give him assistance, not just say "You can do this." For example, he almost certainly needs some one-on-one practice with skipping, hopping, and other physical activities. Once he trusts his teachers, believes that they care about him, and learns the skills he needs to meet his needs appropriately, he will most likely try harder to behave appropriately.

Another crucial step is helping the teachers to become more aware of when Ryan is behaving appropriately. Again, observation is critical. There is a lot of valuable information hidden in these moments, but because the teachers have been focusing on his aggressive behavior and because he hasn't let them come near him, they may not have noticed any of his positive actions. The behavior plan suggests following up his efforts to act appropriately with activities that he likes as well as building the relationship with him. Chances are he enjoys the activities that engage him and those that provide opportunities for him to get on reasonably well with his peers. The teachers could ask the family what he likes to do at home. He may like the calming effect of sand or water play. Would he like story time or circle better if he were sitting next to Lucy or the teacher? If he likes helping, the teachers can organize things he can help with.

FA offers significant clues to challenging behavior, but it's important to remember that it isn't a cure-all and behaviors may have more than one function. Help your teachers to understand the importance of looking at the behavior from the child's point of view. If they can bolster his competence and confidence in one area, then other behaviors may become preventable or even cease completely.

For Further Learning

Books

Dunlap, G. 2016. *Prevent-Teach-Reinforce for Families: A Model of Individualized Positive Behavior Support for Home and Community.* Baltimore, MD: Brookes.

Dunlap, G., & P. Strain. 2013. *Prevent-Teach-Reinforce for Young Children: The Early Childhood Model of Individualized Positive Behavior Support.* Baltimore, MD: Brookes.

Kaiser, B., & J.S. Rasminsky. 2017. *Challenging Behavior in Young Children: Understanding, Preventing, and Responding Effectively.* 4th ed. Columbus, OH: Pearson Education.

Web Resource

National Center for Pyramid Model Innovations (NCPMI): challengingbehavior.cbcs.usf.edu

CHAPTER THIRTEEN

Trauma and Behavior

Four-year-old Wyatt threw things, hit and kicked his peers and teachers, and rarely played with anyone without conflict for more than a few minutes. When his family finally agreed to have him evaluated, they were told by the specialist that he was doing his best to cope with his life circumstances. Since Wyatt was a member of what we assumed to be a loving extended family, no one understood what that meant. We could see nothing particularly hard about his circumstances, and even when we asked, his parents never mentioned any difficulties or trauma. Nonetheless we eventually realized that we had to learn how to respond to his behavior in a trauma-sensitive way.

You've probably heard or read about trauma and new ways of addressing it, and you may even have begun to implement these methods in your own school or center—or you may still be at the stage of wanting to know more. We tell you the story above because your educators probably know that some traumas—such as natural disasters, sexual abuse, placement in multiple foster care homes, living in a violent neighborhood, or fleeing from a war-torn country—have a great impact on children's behavior. But they may not realize that a child who seems to have it all could also be traumatized. And there is usually no way for them to find out.

What Is Trauma?

Betsy Groves, author of *Children Who See Too Much* (2003), defines trauma simply as "any event that undermines a child's sense of physical or emotional safety or poses a threat to the safety of the child's parents or caregivers." Barbara Sorrels (2015), an expert in responding to trauma, describes two types:

> *Acute trauma* is a single overwhelming event that often affects a whole community, such as a hurricane, a fire, a school shooting, or an automobile accident.

> *Complex trauma* is the experience of severe, prolonged, or repetitive adverse events over a period of time without the support of a caring adult, such as living in a home where neglect, physical, emotional, or substance abuse or domestic violence is taking place. This type of trauma is far more difficult to know about and is often mistakenly diagnosed as ADHD.

Trauma in young children is much more pervasive—and much more destructive—than was previously understood. According to the 2016 National Survey of Children's Health, just under half of all children in the United States have experienced at least one potentially traumatic event in the form of an adverse childhood experience (ACE). (See Chapter 2.) One in 10 children has experienced three or more potentially traumatic events, putting them in a category of very high risk for trauma-type effects (Sacks & Murphey 2018).

Children are also at risk of trauma as a result of large and systemic events, such as the COVID-19 pandemic, poverty, racism, homelessness, discrimination, foster care, bullying, repeated medical procedures, life-threatening illness, human-made or natural disasters, or the loss of a caregiver through war, incarceration, abandonment, deportation, migration, or death (Harris 2019).

Furthermore, a great many children experience racial or historical trauma, the "cumulative emotional and psychological wounding as a result of group traumatic experiences transmitted across generations," such as the slavery of Black people and the murder and displacement of Native Americans (National Child Traumatic Stress Network, Justice Consortium, Schools Committee, & Culture Consortium 2017). In these families, each successive generation carries the burdens of the past, whether consciously or unconsciously, and transmits this history in its stories, parenting style, and possibly even via epigenetically marked genes (although the evidence for this is still controversial) (Curry 2019; Youssef et al. 2018) as it strives to protect its children by preparing them to deal with these still very real threats.

As with Wyatt, you and your staff may never know what traumatic experiences a child has been through, but it is important to understand how trauma can affect a child's behavior and how all of you can respond most effectively when a child behaves inappropriately or loses control.

What Can Trauma Do to the Brain?

The brain of a child who's experienced trauma can be quick to perceive any reminder of it as a threat—a new person in the room, an unexpected sound, a harsh tone of voice, someone coming too close—whether or not it's actually threatening and whether or not she's consciously aware of it. The presence of a threat automatically sets off the fight-flight-or-freeze mechanism of the child's stress response system and instantly sends the stress hormone cortisol into her brain and body to protect her. In a normal stress response, the cortisol recedes with the threat. But in a child exposed to trauma, the threat, the fear, and the stress response may remain—along with the cortisol (National Scientific Council on the Developing Child 2010).

If the stress response system is triggered often, intensely, or for long periods, and if there is no caring adult to buffer its effects, the young child's cortisol level remains high, potentially damaging her developing brain, and her stress response system may become harder and harder to turn off. The much-used amygdala, the first responder to threat, may grow stronger and hypervigilant and send out false alarms, shutting down the thinking part of the brain, the prefrontal cortex; the hippocampus, which is involved in memory and information processing and would ordinarily intervene, may remain underdeveloped.

How Does the Fight-Flight-or-Freeze Reaction Affect Children's Behavior?

When a child's fight-flight-or-freeze reaction kicks in, he doesn't have the capacity to think about what he's doing. He fears for his safety, and he just acts. In fight mode, he may scream, kick, bite, or throw himself on the floor. If he's in flight mode, he may hide under a table, cover himself with a blanket, or literally flee by running out of the room. And a child in the freeze state—a common response for infants and toddlers—spaces out, daydreams, or even sleeps (Sorrels 2015).

Because the adults in his life have let him down by failing to protect him from trauma, the child may not trust other people, may have difficulty reading social cues and forming relationships with both peers and adults, likely sees the world as a dangerous place, and may remain in a constant state of fear and anxiety, on guard against possible threats (Statman-Weil 2015). Since his stress response system has prevented the reasoning part of his brain from acting, he may be preoccupied with these threats and unable to concentrate on anything else. As a consequence, he may have trouble learning, paying attention, processing and retrieving information, and controlling his impulses (Harris 2019). His language development, social and emotional regulation, and ability to control his behavior may also be damaged, putting him at high risk for challenging behavior, especially the kind traditionally labeled noncompliant, defiant, oppositional, or aggressive.

However, research on trauma has made it clear that this difficult behavior is not intentional and certainly not a way for a child to say he's the boss, but rather it is driven by fear and is actually a cry for help and a protective strategy for coping with his experience (Sorrels 2015). It is also a means of communication, a method for telling us something is very wrong when he doesn't have the words or the ability to express his distress in any other way.

It is useful to know some of what to expect, even though the behaviors of children who've experienced trauma vary with the child's age; with the type, intensity, and timing of the trauma itself; with the child's personality; and with the quality of support that his family and other caregivers can provide. Infants may

> Be difficult to soothe and comfort

> Resist being held or even being touched

> Show little interest in playing (Sorrels 2015)

Toddlers may demonstrate

> Severe separation anxiety

> Frequent temper tantrums

> Unprovoked aggression

> A withdrawn affect

> Significant language delay

> Play that is random and erratic (Sorrels 2015)

Preschoolers may

> Be hypervigilant

> Become attached indiscriminately, even to acquaintances and total strangers

> Misinterpret facial expressions and body language in a negative way because they may see things through a sense of shame and worthlessness

> Struggle with strong emotions and express anger and frustration through their bodies, becoming prone to unprovoked aggression, particularly in moments of emotional closeness

> Lack play skills, especially if the play involves symbols and language, such as dramatic play

> Try to control everyone and everything in their environment, which helps them to feel safe (Sorrels 2015)

What Can Administrators and Teachers Do?

Many teachers find it difficult to work with children who behave in such unpredictable and problematic ways. The strategies they've used in the past don't work, and they become frustrated and angry. How can you help them to turn things around?

In order to carry out this work, educators have to be aware that trauma is real and can have very serious, lasting effects. Because it influences the way children behave, teachers may also have to learn new ways to prevent and respond to children's inappropriate behavior, especially if they've been trained in behaviorist techniques for addressing it. In an *Education Week* poll, 25 percent of the teachers surveyed confessed that they had trouble finding ways to help students experiencing emotional or psychological distress (Sparks 2019b). On the other hand, teachers may be surprised to discover that it makes sense to assume that every child has a history of trauma (Institute on Trauma and Trauma-Informed Care, n.d.), that best practice for children with trauma is actually best practice for all children, and that all children benefit from a trauma-sensitive approach (Erdman & Colker with Winter 2020; Venet 2018).

Create a Relationship

Once again, addressing challenging behavior is all about building relationships with every child. According to Sorrels, "Children who've been harmed in a relationship can only be healed in a relationship. . . . It is the ongoing, daily interactions with loving, emotionally responsive and caring adults . . . that bring about healing. . . . Because child care providers and teachers often spend more waking hours with a child than any other adult, they are key players in the path to healing" (2015, 8–9). The idea here is to provide a secure base to buffer stress so that children who don't trust anyone can feel safe and protected, know that their needs will be taken care of, learn to trust, and realize that perhaps the world isn't such a bad place after all (Nicholson, Perez, & Kurtz 2019).

However, this is likely to be a difficult task. Some children who've experienced trauma haven't had the opportunity to develop a secure attachment to a caregiver—which is the basis for trust. If no one has consistently loved them and responded to their needs, protected them and provided them with emotional support, or acted as a positive role model to look up to and learn from, they may feel unloved, incompetent, and ashamed. They may even believe they deserve to be treated badly. When a teacher offers them nurturing and warmth, they can feel frightened and vulnerable and use challenging behavior to push her away (Erdman & Colker with Winter 2020). It will take a long time for such children to learn to manage their emotions and form relationships, but in the meantime, they need loving support to reach these goals.

> The teacher noticed that Emiliano was working hard on a complex block structure and went over to encourage him. But as she approached, he curled up into a ball. She assumed he wanted to be left alone and turned away.
>
> But the truth was that Emiliano was protecting himself. Over time the teacher realized that he had difficulty accepting positive recognition, and she looked for ways to gently build his comfort with encouragement, positive reinforcement, or compliments. Using calm, open body language, she showed him that she was still there, hoping he'd soon resume playing and she could give him a thumbs up, a smile, or a nod, say something positive, or ask an open-ended question like "What are you building?"
>
> She knew that if she responded in this way whenever he withdrew from her positive approach, little by little he would be ready for more contact. She had to start where he was.

Develop a New Attitude

In order to create a warm, caring relationship with a child whose behavior is often challenging and unpredictable, teachers may have to make a paradigm shift. Instead of seeing a disobedient, defiant, and angry child who they feel needs to be disciplined, they must reframe their approach to see a scared, anxious child who needs respect, kindness, and compassion and whose development may be far behind her chronological age (Sorrels 2015). With this fresh perspective, her teachers will be able to stop judging her and instead respond to her and her behavior with empathy and flexibility and even strive to make their connection stronger. Rather than asking themselves "What's wrong with this child?," they must start asking "What's happened to this child?" Even if they never know the answer, this attitude can make a big difference.

From the teacher's perspective, a situation may not seem at all threatening, so it's important to remind her that it's the child's view that counts, not the teacher's, and her unconditional positive regard is a vital ingredient in the child's ability to recover from the unspeakable (Wolpow et al. 2009). Even when Wyatt is out of control, a teacher can help him learn new ways of being by showing that she cares and making it clear that Wyatt cannot change the fact that she cares (Platt 2019; Watson with Ecken 2003). As Sorrels writes, "A fundamental principle to remember in dealing with children from hard places is that we need to bring them close rather than push them away when they display inappropriate behavior. The underlying message we want them to hear is that we will love them through their unlovely behavior" (2015, 132).

Help Teachers Learn to Regulate Their Emotions

In response to a teacher's reasonable request, such as telling him to put on his coat to go outside, a child who's experienced trauma may sometimes compulsively and unconsciously lash out in order to recruit the teacher into a reenactment of his trauma (Craig 2016). You need to remind the teacher that if she is going to succeed in calming him, she must communicate a sense of safety and remain calm, collected, and caring herself. Her own behavior can all too easily trigger a child's stress reaction—or calm him down. Emotional states are contagious, brain to brain, and whenever a teacher interacts with a child, the mirror neurons in their brains automatically synchronize their feelings (Aalto University 2012; Goleman 2006).

Under these circumstances, a teacher's most valuable—indeed indispensable—asset is her own self-regulation, that is, her ability to "stay calm and regulated and to manage her own internal emotional state" (Nicholson, Perez, & Kurtz 2019) and at the same time to remain emotionally available to the child. This state of mind is necessary because it

› Reassures the child that it's okay to have strong emotions and they won't scare away his teacher or destroy their relationship

› Prevents the teacher's negative emotions—fear, distress, anger, frustration—from triggering a child's stress response and intensifying his challenging behavior

› Helps the child learn to tolerate his own uneasy feelings and eventually to take charge of them himself

You can help your teachers to gain control of their emotions by reminding them privately that feelings are contagious and how important it is for them to project their strong, caring, calm feelings for the child rather than allowing the child's fear, distress, and chaos to be communicated to them (Nicholson, Perez, & Kurtz 2019). They can do this by maintaining a gentle and positive tone of voice, a calm facial expression, a comfortable distance from the child, and a relaxed posture (arms at their sides, hands not on their hips!) and by trying to understand what the child is feeling underneath his behavior (Desautels 2019). They can also use the calming techniques they learned to deal with an amygdala hijack, such as taking five deep breaths or doing a simple arithmetic problem in their head (see Chapters 5 and 10). In this way, they can prevent the child from reacting defensively, lead him back into a competent state, and help him to develop new, healthier brain pathways (Nicholson, Perez, & Kurtz 2019).

Help Educators to Teach Children Self-Regulation

When the teacher and child have a strong relationship, the teacher can buffer the child's stress by validating his feelings and responding positively and empathically. Such a response gives the child a chance to acquire new skills. Emphasize how important it is for the teacher not to take things personally but to help the child learn to focus on one of the many sensations, thoughts, feelings, and images going on inside his body. Instead of concentrating on his fear, he can pay attention to how his body feels, identify those feelings, and think about how to put them into words (Craig 2016; Erdman & Colker with Winter 2020).

Teachers can do this by identifying and talking about their own feelings and the feelings of the other children and by reading books and singing songs about feelings. They can also use feeling charts, point out how faces look when they're mad or sad or scared or happy, have the children draw and make feeling faces, look at each other's faces to see how each feeling appears, and talk about what makes them feel that way. This will enable the child who has trouble with empathy to learn how others feel and that people don't always feel the same way about things.

Language should have a prominent place in all classroom interactions because children who've experienced trauma often lack the language skills and words that can provide them with an appropriate way to tell others how they feel (Craig 2016). It's important to read books about strong feelings, shared experiences, or trauma-related subjects to individual children as well as to the whole group (Erdman & Colker with Winter 2020).

Children exposed to trauma often don't recognize the connection between an act and its emotional effect and the difference between accidental and on purpose. For example, when Marco trips and bumps into Wyatt, Wyatt kicks him because he's sure Marco pushed him on purpose. The teacher should help Wyatt understand the difference between intentional and accidental, explain that kicking hurts, discuss possible alternatives, and encourage Wyatt to think about how he could make Marco feel better. All of this tells children that everyone has feelings, that it's all right to express them, and that they're normal and manageable.

Self-soothing activities are also extremely helpful, so encourage your teachers to make the sand and water tables and playdough available, play soothing music, and encourage deep breathing (smell the flowers, blow out the candle, blow bubbles). Teachers can also utilize fidgets and stress balls to help keep children calm and use large motor and rough-and-tumble play to bolster their underdeveloped ability to read social cues.

Mindfulness is an effective tool for dealing with toxic stress and trauma (Ortiz & Sibinga 2017). It boosts resilience, attention, working memory, and impulse control and tamps down reactions like fear and anger (see Chapter 6). At the same time, it shows children that even if they can't change a situation, at least they can control how they react to it (Craig 2016). But remember: sometimes asking children who've been exposed to trauma to close their eyes or sit in a certain way can trigger a stress response, so pay close attention and respond flexibly to children's preferences and reactions (Mindshift 2019).

Create a Safe, Predictable Environment

As always, prevention is the best intervention, and this is especially true for children who've experienced trauma. Consistency is the key. Help your teachers to develop stable, predictable school and classroom environments where children feel safe and in control with these strategies:

> Create and maintain explicit and consistent routines and procedures, and explain, model, rehearse, and practice them with the class so that everyone knows what to do at every step.

> Provide timers, hourglasses, and visual schedules and clues (such as carpet squares and footprints on the floor) so that the children know exactly what's coming next, how much time they have, and where to sit or stand.

> Reduce the number of transitions and stay close at hand to coach the children as they move from one place or activity to another.

> Build a sense of community and give children a chance to see collaboration and respect for others at work in class meetings and circle time (Craig 2016), and notice and reinforce any positive contribution a child makes to the group.

> Equip their classrooms with a cozy, tranquil space, furnished with washable pillows, soft light, blankets, stuffed animals, books, and music, where children can go when they need to calm down and collect themselves. (Nicholson, Perez, & Kurtz 2019)

Eliminate Triggers

Help your staff to become sensitive to triggers in the environment and work to eliminate them as much as possible. To begin with, this means abolishing time-out, public reprimands, and aversive consequences, which don't give children who've experienced trauma the emotional support they need but rather teach them it's okay to use power to control others, thus confirming they're right not to trust. Even if the teacher's actions are directed toward another child, they will still have an impact on Wyatt's feelings of trust and safety.

A teacher of 3- and 4-year-olds heard that a new child, Haruki, was coming to her group from an area recently devastated by forest fires. His family had found a place to stay, but they enrolled him in the early learning program so that they could get their lives in order. Haruki clung to his mother when she tried to drop him off, and he didn't want to play with the other children or participate in activities. When the class was outdoors, he screamed and threw himself onto the ground.

The teacher realized that her first priority was to develop Haruki's trust, so rather than reprimand him or dole out consequences, she quickly arranged to spend time talking alone with him. She told him she was scared when the fires started but felt better now. Haruki replied that he was still scared and sad and worried about where his family would go next. But he was soon playing "I Spy" with the teacher, and when she asked Haruki if he wanted to sit beside her and listen to a story she would read to everyone, he took her hand and they joined the other children.

Preventing possible triggers also means eliminating surprises and unnecessary change and telling children when something unusual is about to occur, such as a field trip or an outside visitor ("Since we've been talking about trains, planes, and automobiles, after circle this morning Lorenzo's mom, who is a pilot, is going to visit and talk with us about what makes a plane fly").

Teachers also need to identify and anticipate difficult periods when children might need extra support. Nap time is hard for many children, but for a child who's experienced trauma it may be even harder. If a child has trouble settling down at nap time, she may be feeling unsafe because abuse and domestic violence may take place when she's in bed at home. Since the teachers can't know whether this is the case, remind them that it's best practice to focus on the signs she's showing, and instead of getting cross, help her to feel protected by putting her cot near an adult she trusts, asking her if she wants a back rub (it's always imperative to ask a child's permission to touch her), allowing her to sleep with a transitional object, or giving her books to look at or headphones for listening to music (Sorrels 2015).

Teachers must be wary of making assumptions, but if they have concrete information, they may be better able to connect the dots and see a pattern between what they know (a 5-year-old child is currently in his fourth foster home) and the child's behavior (he is throwing chairs). This may allow them to understand the meaning of the behavior at the moment when it occurs (Nicholson, Perez, & Kurtz 2019).

Because fear frequently rules the lives of children exposed to trauma, they may have a strong need to control the environment and the people around them. As a result, they feel vulnerable when they are expected to follow others' rules or requests and may react unpredictably when a teacher uses an authoritative manner to direct their behavior. Remind your teachers that it is always preferable to offer a choice when giving directions or telling children what to do. This approach is more likely to secure their cooperation because it gives them a sense of control and empowerment. Explaining the reasons for the request before making it is also helpful (Minahan 2019).

The Collaborative and Proactive Solutions (CPS) model, discussed in Chapter 11, relies on a strong teacher–child relationship and can help a child feel that she is being heard and teach her how to reach a compromise—and prevent a stress response or a power struggle. When teachers remember to slow things down, extend the time to comply with directions, speak privately with the child, and give her space to do what's asked, the pressure to respond immediately is removed and children often do the right thing.

All children need opportunities to understand their reality on their own terms. In the dramatic play area, younger children can have control, make their own rules, and explore events and emotions, giving them a safe way to master things and build competence and confidence. Long stretches of uninterrupted play provide the opportunity to process their anxiety, fear, and sadness and enable them to create safe outcomes, such as bringing in helpers like doctors and ambulances, although they may need assistance when it comes to thinking up positive endings. As Sorrels (2015) points out, when children control their own play, they make it only as intense as they can handle. In any case, it's important for teachers to monitor what's going on so that they can help when necessary or volunteer to act as play partners. Children can also make order from chaos by playing with blocks, LEGOs, or magnetic blocks.

Older children need these opportunities as well. They may benefit from expressing themselves through art activities or through creating their own stories, plays, or dances. Even in primary school, every child should have a chance to explore her world in her own way. With creativity, teachers can integrate these artistic endeavors into the demands of the existing curriculum, but you need to emphasize the importance of providing the opportunity.

Implement a Strengths-Based Approach

It's important for your teachers to remember that trauma isn't the only thing in the lives of children who've experienced it and doesn't define them (Nicholson, Perez, & Kurtz 2019). Like all children, they have strengths, needs, interests, and even resiliencies of their own. If the teacher's eyes are trained exclusively on the child's difficult behavior, those positive qualities may be hard to see.

Remind your staff to watch for moments when children's behavior isn't challenging, interests that they have, and things that they do well and to incorporate these into the curriculum. It will take time and practice for children exposed to trauma to learn that their own ideas and needs matter, and they—and your teachers—need to remember that the learning process is full of mistakes and reversals. Advise your staff to talk less, listen more, and ask how they can help (Rossen 2019).

Teach Friendship Skills

It's hard for children who have experienced trauma to make friends. They have a tendency to reject or push away their peers in the same way that they reject or push away their teachers, and they often don't have the skills necessary to enter groups or even to play one-on-one. But these relationships are important to their well-being, and you should encourage your teachers to help develop them.

In *Trauma and Young Children*, Sarah Erdman and Laura Colker (with Winter 2020) offer teachers these suggestions:

> "Model being a friend and what you like about being a friend." (53)
> Use mirrors, posters, and books to help children learn to read facial cues.
> Accompany and coach children when they try to enter activities.
> Match up children to play and work together on projects (an especially good tactic when the child exposed to trauma can be a leader).
> Sit privately with a child who's been rejected to discuss what happened and what he can do next time.

Teach Problem Solving

Children who've experienced trauma may often know just one way to solve problems, and that is with aggression. Educators need to help children feel confident about their problem-solving skills and teach them to use calming techniques before they react, such as counting to five or using the Turtle Technique (Robin, Schneider, & Dolnick 1976; Webster-Stratton 1991). (For Further Learning.)

When there is a problem between children, the conflict resolution process is an effective way to reach a peaceful solution, but it requires empathy—an understanding of others' thoughts and feelings—which children exposed to trauma may not have acquired. Teachers should work with the whole class to develop the children's ability to put themselves in someone else's shoes, reinforcing signs of empathy among the children and paying particular attention to those who need a bit of extra help. (See Chapters 6 and 11.)

When the children are calm, they can begin to learn and practice the basic steps of problem solving with the teacher as a guide:

> Each child takes a turn to say what he feels. Conflict usually starts with a feeling of anger, disappointment, or frustration, and these feelings must be identified and acknowledged.

> With the teacher's help, the children define their problem as one they share and that actually has a potential solution: "There aren't enough markers for everyone!"

> Both children think of possible solutions: "We can get more markers." The teacher can encourage them by saying "That's one idea. What's another?"— to which they might respond, "We can share the markers."

> They try to foresee what will happen if they use their ideas, examining each idea's pros and cons. "If we share the markers we need to sit closer. If we get more markers we can have more space."

> Finally, they choose what looks like the best solution and try it. "Let's get more markers so we can work on big pieces of paper."

Remind your teachers to check in later to see how things are going.

Help Teachers to Develop Their Resilience

Because it involves so many powerful emotions, working with children with challenging behavior and especially those who've experienced trauma is probably the most stressful aspect of the teaching profession. It obliges teachers to be resilient: to be able to cope with difficult situations, to meet their own needs, to have a positive attitude, and to see challenges as a way to grow and learn ("Wyatt is really having a hard time today. Tomorrow I'm going to make sure he feels supported. I know I have the skills to help him do better").

However, having a positive, resilient response under such difficult conditions is no piece of cake. How, then, should you and your teachers proceed? First, there is no doubt that learning about trauma's effects on children is the foundation. All staff need to know—and really believe—that a child with this very challenging behavior is not out to get them; that his behavior is born out of fear, not malice; and above all, as we keep repeating, that it is not to be taken personally. It is, in fact, his strategy for coping with his trauma and adversity (Craig 2016).

Probably just as important is everyone's capacity to take care of themselves. This means such obvious things as eating and sleeping well, exercising, and taking time for nurturing, whether by being with family and friends, pursuing a hobby or sport, doing the crossword puzzle, taking short naps, or just relaxing and having fun (Harris 2019). Cultivating and maintaining relationships is particularly vital—we all need someone to talk to who listens and doesn't judge.

All the people associated with the program, including you, also need to know themselves well—to be aware of their beliefs, button pushers, triggers, biases, and privileges—so that they can manage their own feelings (National Child Traumatic Stress Network, Justice Consortium, Schools Committee, & Culture Consortium 2017) and better understand the children's emotions and reactions. Self-reflection, self-awareness, mindfulness, and keeping a journal are all keys to this process. (See Chapter 5.)

Secondary Trauma

Unfortunately, there may be times when you or a member of your staff becomes totally overwhelmed by this difficult work. You and your teachers may know that you're feeling exceptionally stressed and exhausted, but you don't always realize that these symptoms are a common reaction to working with someone who's been exposed to trauma. This condition goes by several names—secondary traumatic stress (STS), vicarious trauma, and compassion fatigue (Erdman & Colker with Winter 2020).

STS may make it difficult to respond effectively to a child with challenging behavior. You may notice that a teacher is increasingly angry or impatient with the children, that she's having trouble focusing or planning activities, that she seems numb or detached, or even that she thinks that trauma has nothing to do with her own or the children's behavior.

In addition, she may have less visible symptoms, such as

> Being jumpy and hypervigilant

> Withdrawing from friends and family

> Feeling anxious or unsafe or incompetent

> Having physical problems like overeating, eating too little, nightmares, or trouble sleeping

> Feeling helpless or guilty about not doing enough

> Either avoiding children who've experienced trauma or worrying continually about them, even when at home or asleep (HHS & ACF, n.d.)

It is extremely important for you to help your teachers acknowledge, appreciate, and address the reality and impact of STS.

Adult Risk Factors

In Chapter 2 we saw how adverse childhood experiences (ACEs) may manifest themselves as children's challenging behavior. But ACEs also have a tremendous impact on the adult lives of those who've experienced adversity as children (CDC, n.d. a). Any of your teachers who experienced ACEs or trauma as a youngster is probably more vulnerable to STS. Her history may remain her secret, but she may still be dealing with the effects of those events and may find it difficult to assist children with challenging behavior. When she recognizes the characteristics of trauma in a child or another adult, some of her own feelings and memories may reappear and make her more empathetic—or, if she has been denying or downplaying the influence of her past on who she is today, she may be more detached and less empathetic. She may even be especially prone to amygdala hijacks.

If you or your staff are interested, you can find your ACEs score at https://acestoohigh.com/got-your-ace-score. This must be a personal choice, and each individual should decide for herself if she wants to know or share her score with you or her colleagues. If anyone on your staff decides to go this route, your active, nonjudgmental listening is crucial.

How You Can Address STS

STS is both preventable and treatable, and addressing it is essential to protecting the quality of care you offer to children and families and the health and well-being of your educators. It's important to educate your teachers about STS and its symptoms so that they can recognize it and understand that it's a normal risk for anyone working with children and families who've experienced trauma. The risk is higher for women, individuals who are highly empathetic, and as we've seen, for anyone with unresolved personal trauma (Meyers & Cornille 2002).

Too often, teachers feel that they are working alone. For those experiencing STS, this can be particularly dangerous since these feelings can easily exacerbate their sense of being overwhelmed, isolated, and without hope. You must make it clear that such symptoms are not a sign of weakness or incompetence but an indicator that they might need support. If you're aware that a teacher has unresolved trauma and doesn't have an adequate support system of her own, be sure to help her find counseling with a professional who knows about trauma.

Peer support groups and reflective supervision are effective strategies for combatting STS. Provide opportunities for your staff to work together. If possible, bring in a mental health professional who's an expert on trauma to help them talk about their feelings on a regular basis so that they can process their emotions, understand their stress responses, and gain skills to cope with STS. According to one teacher in a center with monthly reflective supervision sessions, "It makes us better teachers because we're not carrying [our stress] inside. We're able to release it" (Einhorn 2019). Professional development and policies that support self-care help to build resilience as well.

In this way, you can create a culture that normalizes the effects of working with children who've experienced trauma (HHS & ACF, n.d.).

Choosing Trauma-Sensitive Care

Leaders can help to create a trauma-sensitive program by consistently using best practices as well as providing the following:

> Professional development that enables staff to understand what trauma is and how it affects children's behavior, including what it can do to their brains—hence to their learning, attention, information processing, language development, and social and emotional skills

> Professional development that offers classroom management techniques focusing on emotional regulation and opportunities for staff to participate in workshops on mindfulness, stress management, and relaxation (Craig 2016)

> A guidance policy that eliminates practices that trigger stress responses (such as time-out) and replaces them with practices that encourage curiosity rather than judgment (see Chapter 4); helps children to repair any physical or emotional harm their behavior has caused rather than punishing or isolating them (Craig 2016); and includes program-wide social and emotional learning

> A school climate that fosters collaboration and mutual support

> Schedules that enable teachers to give each other breaks when necessary and to meet to discuss problems and solutions in staff meetings and professional learning communities (Craig 2016)

> A relationship with community mental health services that can be available to your educators as well as to the children and families

Early childhood educators struggle to find ways to understand, prevent, and respond effectively to children's challenging behavior, and they look to you to guide and support them. Whether the behavior is a response to trauma, temperament, teaching styles, or classroom culture, you play a very important role. Your ability to create partnerships with families and collaboration among teachers is key, and you can achieve these goals by continuing to pursue the knowledge, experience, and commitment you need to provide the best possible support and training for everyone.

For Further Learning

Books

Alexander, J. 2019. *Building Trauma-Sensitive Schools: Your Guide to Creating Safe, Supportive Learning Environments for All Students*. Baltimore, MD: Brookes.

Erdman, S., & L.J. Colker. With E.C. Winter. 2020. *Trauma and Young Children: Teaching Strategies to Support and Empower*. Washington, DC: NAEYC.

Nicholson, J., L. Perez, & J. Kurtz. 2019. *Trauma-Informed Practices for Early Childhood Educators: Relationship-Based Approaches that Support Healing and Build Resilience in Young Children*. New York: Routledge.

Sorrels, B. 2015. *Reaching and Teaching Children Exposed to Trauma*. Lewisville, NC: Gryphon House.

Web Resource

Lentini, R., L.N. Giroux, & M.L. Hemmeter. 2019. *Tucker Turtle Takes Time to Tuck and Think*. https://challengingbehavior.cbcs.usf.edu/docs/TuckerTurtle_Story.pdf.

Appendices

Sample Guidance Policy

ABC Center | Guidance and Discipline

Working with Children's Challenging Behavior

Professionals who work with young children expect to be met with challenging behavior from time to time. During the first five years of life, children are just beginning to learn how to handle their own intense emotions and conform to the behavioral expectations of society. As parents and teachers know, this is a lengthy process.

In our early care and education setting, we define challenging behavior as any behavior that

> Interferes with children's learning, development and success at play

> Is harmful to the child, other children or adults

> Puts a child at high risk for later social problems or school failure

It can be direct (e.g., hitting, pushing, biting, kicking) or indirect (e.g., teasing, ignoring rules or instructions, excluding others, name calling, destroying objects, having temper tantrums).

The ABC staff sees working with children's challenging behavior as an integral aspect of our job. The word *discipline* has, as its root meaning, "instruction" or "training." This meaning, rather than punishment, is the foundation for our approach to guiding children's behavior. We accept that young children will sometimes display their emotions or try to achieve their goals in unproductive or immature ways. That is simply part of being very young. Much of children's most valuable learning, especially in a group setting, occurs in the course of behavioral problem solving. The approaches we use vary by age group, but have the following elements in common:

> **Adults model positive behavior.** We show that we can accept, control and express feelings in direct and non-aggressive ways; we let children know that we are not afraid of their intense emotions and will not punish, threaten or withdraw from them.

> **Teachers design the physical environment to minimize conflict.** We provide multiples of toys and materials for groups of children, define classroom and outdoor areas clearly to allow for both active and quiet play and strive to maintain an appropriately calm level of stimulation.

> **Teachers maintain age-appropriate expectations for children's behavior.** We attempt to minimize unreasonable waiting and transition times, and limit the length of large group and teacher-directed activity times according to children's developmental levels. We give children large blocks of uninterrupted time during which to make their own activity choices.

> **Teachers establish simple rules, or expectations, for the classroom community.** Older preschool children participate in this process early in the school year. When issues arise, adults and children can reference the "Be safe, Be kind, Be respectful" guidelines as reminders about what kinds of behavior facilitate life in a group setting.

> **Adults closely observe and supervise children's activities and interactions.** With our high ratios of adults to children and our emphasis on attentive observation, we can often intervene to guide children before situations escalate.

> **Adults help children verbalize their feelings, frustrations and concerns.** The staff will help children describe problems, generate possible solutions, and think through logical consequences of their actions. Even babies will hear their caregivers describing actions, problems, solutions and logical consequences. The adult role is to be a helper in positive problem solving. We want children to value cooperation and teamwork. We help them to learn peaceful, productive approaches to interacting.

> **Children whose behavior endangers others will be temporarily supervised away from other children.** This is not the same as the practice of using a "time-out" (the traditional chair in the corner) for a child. An adult will help the child move away from a group situation. The child will then process the problem verbally with the staff member and any other concerned parties. An adult will stay close to any child who is emotionally out of control and needs private time to regain composure.

> **Discipline, i.e., guidance, will always be positive, productive and immediate when behavior is inappropriate.** No child will be humiliated, shamed, frightened, coerced or subjected to physical punishment or verbal or physical abuse by any staff member, student, or volunteer working in the ABC program. Every member of the ABC professional staff understands and follows our disciplinary approach as well as the standards on guidance and management in our state licensing regulations. We work intensively with our student caregivers so that they also understand and employ this guidance approach.

> **When a pattern of behavior persists that endangers self, others or property, or significantly disrupts the program, we will work with a child's family to find solutions, up to and including referral for outside services or exclusion from the ECL program.** Exclusion will always be a last resort, after all other possible interventions have been exhausted and there is agreement that a different setting is in the best interest of the child. In that circumstance, the program will offer assistance to the family in accessing services and an alternative placement. Our actions will always comply with federal and state civil rights laws.

Adapted, by permission, from "Guidance and Discipline Policy: Working with Children's Challenging Behavior" (Early Childhood Lab School, Center for Child and Family Studies, University of California, Davis). https://ccfs.ucdavis.edu/guidance-and-discipline-policy

Behavior Incident Report

Child's Name _____ Date _____

Child's age/gender/race _____

Home language _____

Length of time child has been at the school/center _____

Behavior _____

Teacher(s) _____

Time of day _____ Activity _____

Location if outside the classroom _____

What could have triggered the behavior? _____

What was going on just before the incident took place? _____

Who was there? _____

What were they doing or saying? _____

What happened during the incident (behaviors)?

What did the child do and say?	How did others respond?

How did the incident end (maintaining consequences)?

What could have been the goal, purpose, or function of the behavior?

Observed by_____

Blank A-B-C Observation Chart

Child's name _____

Date	Activity/Teacher	Antecedent	Behavior	Maintaining Consequence	Possible Function

Ryan's A-B-C Observation Chart

Child's name ___Ryan___

Date	Activity/Teacher	Antecedent	Behavior	Maintaining Consequence	Possible Function
Monday, Dec. 11	Circle/Latoya	Starting a new song	Kicks, pinches child beside him	Told to keep hands to himself	Attention from teacher
		Everyone is singing	Pinches and hits child beside him	Told to leave circle and look at a book. He leaves	Escape the activity
	Getting ready to go outside/Latoya	Struggling with his shoes	Throws shoes across the room	Teacher picks up the shoes and offers her help	Attention from teacher
	Gross motor hopping and jumping across the yard	Everyone is getting a turn in small groups	Yells and pushes Jon	Teacher removes him from group to sit and watch	Escape from activity
Thursday, Dec. 14	Art activity/Latoya	Started work, looked around at other children's work	Dumps the glue on the table and pushes his chair over	Teacher removes him from the activity	Escape from activity
	Storytime/Mike	Teacher starts reading	Gets up on his knees so other children cannot see	Teacher tells him to sit down	Attention from teacher
Friday, Dec. 15	Arrival/Maya	Other children involved in a variety of activities	Walks to block area and knocks over structure	Children yell at him	Attention from peers
	Circle time/Latoya	Playing "Bug in a Rug"	Hits child beside him	Teacher asks him to leave circle. He leaves	Escape from activity
	Lunch time/Latoya	Teacher reminds him that it is his turn to pour the milk	He pushes over his chair and kicks it	Teacher places him at a table by himself with his lunch and a glass of milk	Escape from pouring the milk

Ryan's Behavior Support Planning Chart

Child's name ___Ryan___

Antecedent	Behavior	Maintaining Consequence
> Small and large motor activities > Circle time > Joining in play with peers	> Hits, pushes, throws objects, kicks, pinches, knocks over blocks and chairs	> Removed from activity > Given an alternative activity
	Function > Escape	

Preventions	Goals/Skills	New Responses
Modify: > Task length > Expectations > Materials **Provide:** > Choices > Teacher and peer support and partnering **Reinforce:** > Approximations of appropriate behavior > Follow least preferred activity with most preferred	**Long term:** > Ryan will be able to participate in all activities successfully. **Short term:** > When asked to participate in an activity that he feels is too difficult, Ryan will ask for help. > When Ryan does not want to participate, he will ask to leave the activity.	**To challenging behavior:** > Let Ryan know his behavior is not safe, teach skills to ask for help or to leave activity, offer assistance, scaffold, identify feelings with words. **To use of new skill:** > Recognize Ryan's effort and persistence. Follow up with a favorite activity.

Adapted, by permission, from L. Fox and M.A. Duda, "Positive Behavior Support" (Technical Assistance Center on Social Emotional Intervention for Young Children). www.challengingbehavior.org

REFERENCES

Aalto University. 2012. "Synchronized Brains: Feeling Strong Emotions Makes People's Brains 'Tick Together.'" ScienceDaily, May 24. www.sciencedaily.com/releases/2012/05/120524112342.htm.

Aces Too High. "Got Your ACE Score?" n.d. *ACES Too High News*. Accessed October 13, 2019. www.acestoohigh.com/got-your-ace-score.

Aguilar, E. 2011. "Coaching Teachers: What You Need to Know." *Education Week Teacher*, February 16. www.edweek.org/tm/articles/2011/02/15/tln_coaching.html.

Aguilar, E. 2017. "12 Ways to Boost Resilience in New Teachers." *Education Week Teacher* (blog), August 14. www.blogs.edweek.org/teachers/coaching_teachers/2017/08/12_ways_to_boost_resilience_in.html.

Aguilar, E. 2018. "The Arc of a Coaching Conversation: Six Steps to More Effective Meetings." *Education Week Teacher* (blog), November 15. www.blogs.edweek.org/teachers/coaching_teachers/2018/11/the_arc_of_a_coaching_conversation.html.

Aguilar, E. 2019. "Getting Mindful About Race in Schools." *Educational Leadership* 76 (7): 62–67.

Aguilar, E. 2017. "Coaching Teachers Through Unexpected Change." *Education Week Teacher* (blog), May 11. www.blogs.edweek.org/teachers/coaching_teachers/2017/05/coaching_teachers_through_unex.html.

Aguilar, E. n.d. "Power Strategies for Strong Emotions." Accessed May 3, 2019. www.blogs.edweek.org/teachers/coaching_teachers/three%20power%20strategies%20for%20dealing%20with%20strong%20emotions.pdf.

Ainsworth, M.D.S., M. Blehar, E. Waters, & S. Wall. 1978. *Patterns of Attachment: A Psychological Study of the Strange Situation*. Hillsdale, NJ: Erlbaum.

Ansari, A., & E. Gershoff. 2015. "Parent Involvement in Head Start and Children's Development: Indirect Effects Through Parenting." *Journal of Marriage and Family* 78 (2): 562–79.

Archer, J., & S. Côté. 2005. "Sex Differences in Aggressive Behavior: A Developmental and Evolutionary Perspective." In *Developmental Origins of Aggression*, eds. R.E. Tremblay, W.W. Hartup, & J. Archer, 425–443. New York: Guilford Press.

Baillargeon, R.H., M. Zoccolillo, K. Keenan, S. Côté, D. Pérusse, H.-X. Wu, M. Boivan, & R. Tremblay. 2007. "Gender Differences in Physical Aggression: A Prospective Population-Based Survey of Children Before and After 2 Years of Age." *Developmental Psychology,* 43 (1): 13–26.

Benedict, R. 1934. "Anthropology and the Abnormal." *Journal of General Psychology* 10: 59–79. https://users.manchester.edu/facstaff/ssnaragon/online/texts/201/benedict,%20anthropology.pdf.

Berg, J.H. 2019. "Leading Together/Toward Shared Instructional Leadership." *Educational Leadership* 76 (6): 86–87. www.ascd.org/publications/educational-leadership/mar19/vol76/num06/Toward-Shared-Instructional-Leadership.aspx.

Berkowicz, J., & A. Myers. 2016. "Four Steps to Leading Successful Change." *Education Week* (blog), July 14. http://blogs.edweek.org/edweek/leadership_360/2016/07/4_steps_to_leading_successful_change.html.

Berkowicz, J., & A. Myers. 2017a. "How Teachers and Students Both Can Prevent Successful Outcomes." *Education Week* (blog), August 13. https://blogs.edweek.org/edweek/leadership_360/2017/08/how_teachers_and_students_both_can_prevent_successful_outcomes.html.

Berkowicz, J., & A. Myers. 2017b. "Student Achievement Depends upon Faculty Relationships and Trusted Leaders." *Education Week* (blog), August 20. https://blogs.edweek.org/edweek/leadership_360/2017/08/student_achievement_depends_upon_faculty_relationships_and_trusted_leaders.html.

Bierman, K.L. 1986. "Process of Change During Social Skills Training with Preadolescents and Its Relation to Treatment Outcomes." *Child Development* 57 (1): 230–40.

Biermeyer, M.A. 2015. "Inspired by Reggio Emilia: Emergent Curriculum in Relationship-Driven Learning Environments." *Young Children* 70 (5): 72–79. www.naeyc.org/resources/pubs/yc/nov2015/emergent-curriculum.

Bijou, S.W., R.F. Peterson, & M.H. Ault. 1968. "A Method to Integrate Descriptive and Experimental Field Studies at the Level of Data and Empirical Concepts." *Journal of Applied Behavior Analysis* 1 (2): 175–91.

Blad, E. 2016. "Nurturing Growth Mindsets: Six Tips from Carol Dweck." *Education Week* (blog), March 14. https://blogs.edweek.org/edweek/rulesforengagement/2016/03/nurturing_growth_mindsets_six_tips_from_carol_dweck.html.

Bloom, P.J. 1991. *Blueprint for Action: Achieving Center-Based Change Through Staff Development*. Mt. Rainier, MD: Gryphon House.

Bloom, P.J. 2004. "Leadership as a Way of Thinking." *ZERO TO THREE* 25 (2): 21–26.

Bloom, P.J. 2007. *From the Inside Out: The Power of Reflection and Self-Awareness*. 2nd ed. Lake Forest, IL: New Horizons.

Bloom, P.J. 2014. *Leadership in Action: How Effective Directors Get Things Done*. 2nd ed. Lake Forest, IL: New Horizons.

Bloom, P.J. 2015. *Blueprint for Action: Leading Our Team in Continuous Quality Improvement*. 3rd ed. Lake Forest, IL: New Horizons.

Bloom, P.J., A. Hentschel, & J. Bella. 2013. *Inspiring Peak Performance: Competence, Commitment, and Collaboration.* Lake Forest, IL: New Horizons.

Bloom, P.J., A. Hentschel, & J. Bella. 2016. *A Great Place to Work: Creating a Healthy Organizational Climate.* 2nd ed. Lake Forest, IL: New Horizons.

Bowlby, J. [1969] 1982. *Attachment and Loss: Vol. 1. Attachment.* New York: Basic Books.

Bradshaw, C.P., E.T. Pas, J.H. Bottiani, W.M. Reinke, K.C. Herman, & M.S. Rosenberg. 2018. "Promoting Cultural Responsivity and Student Engagement Through Double Check Coaching of Classroom Teachers: An Efficacy Study." *School Psychology Review* 47 (2): 118–34.

Briggs-Gowan, M.J., J.D. Ford, L. Fraleigh, K. McCarthy, & A.S. Carter. 2010. "Prevalence of Exposure to Potentially Traumatic Events in a Healthy Birth Cohort of Very Young Children in the Northeastern United States." *Journal of Traumatic Stress* 23 (6): 725–33.

British Columbia Day Care Action Coalition & Early Childhood Educators of British Columbia. 2016. *Guiding Children's Behaviour.* www2.gov.bc.ca/assets/gov/health/about-bc-s-health-care-system/child-day-care/guiding_childrens_behaviour_april_2017.pdf.

Broidy, L.M., D.S. Nagin, R.E. Tremblay, J.E. Bates, B. Brame, K.A. Dodge, D. Fergusson, J.L. Horwood, R. Loeber, R. Laird, D.R. Lynam, T.E. Moffitt, G.S. Pettit, & F. Vitaro. 2003. "Developmental Trajectories of Childhood Disruptive Behaviors and Adolescent Delinquency: A Six-Site, Cross-National Study." *Developmental Psychology* 39 (2) 222–45.

Brummelman, S. Thomaes, G. Overbeek, O. De Castro, M.A. Van Den Hout, & B. Bushman. 2013. "On Feeding Those Hungry for Praise: Person Praise Backfires in Children with Low Self-Esteem." *Journal of Experimental Psychology* 143: 9–14.

Bruno, H.E. 2012. *What You Need to Lead an Early Childhood Program: Emotional Intelligence in Practice.* Washington, DC: NAEYC.

Burden, P. 2017. *Classroom Management: Creating a Successful K–12 Learning Community.* 6th ed. Hoboken, NJ: Wiley.

Butchard, N., & R. Spencler. 2011. *Working Effectively with Violent and Aggressive States.* Winnipeg, MB: WEVAS.

Campbell, S.B. 2006. "Maladjustment in Preschool Children: A Developmental Psychopathology Perspective." In *Handbook of Early Childhood Development*, eds. K. McCartney & D. Phillips, 357–77. Malden, MA: Blackwell.

Card, N.A., B.D. Stucky, G.M. Sawalani, & T.D. Little. 2008. "Direct and Indirect Aggression During Childhood and Adolescence: A Meta-Analytic Review of Gender Differences, Intercorrelations, and Relations to Maladjustments." *Child Development* 79 (5): 1185–229.

Cardichon, J., & L. Darling-Hammond. 2019. "Protecting Students' Civil Rights: The Federal Role in School Discipline." Learning Policy Institute, May. https://learningpolicyinstitute.org/sites/default/files/product-files/Federal_Role_School_Discipline_REPORT.pdf.

Carey, W.B. 2017. "Editorial Perspective: Whatever Happened to Temperament?" *Journal of Child Psychology and Psychiatry* 58 (12): 1381–82. https://acamh.onlinelibrary.wiley.com/doi/pdf/10.1111/jcpp.12816.

Carter, M. 2016. "What Do Teachers Need Most from Their Directors?" In *Leading Early Childhood Organizations,* 60–64. The Art of Leadership Series. Redmond, WA: Exchange Press.

Carter, M., & D. Curtis. 2010. *The Visionary Director: A Handbook for Dreaming, Organizing, and Improvising in Your Center.* 2nd ed. St. Paul, MN: Redleaf Press.

Caspi, A., & P.A. Silva. 1995. "Temperamental Qualities at Age Three Predict Personality Traits in Young Adulthood: Longitudinal Evidence from a Birth Cohort." *Child Development* 66 (2): 486–98.

Caspi, A., B.W. Roberts, & R.L. Shiner. 2005. "Personality Development: Stability and Change." *Annual Review of Psychology* 56: 17.1–17.32.

CDC (Centers for Disease Control and Prevention). n.d. a. "Professional Development: Follow-Up Support Tool Kit." Accessed May 3, 2019. www.cdc.gov/healthyschools/tths/followup_toolkit-508.pdf.

CDC (Centers for Disease Control and Prevention). n.d. b. "About the CDC-Kaiser ACE Study." Accessed April 13, 2020. www.cdc.gov/violenceprevention/acestudy/about.html.

Chandler, L.K., C.M. Dahlquist, A.C. Repp, & C. Feltz. 1999. "The Effects of Team-Based Functional Assessment on the Behavior of Students in Classroom Settings." *Exceptional Children* 66 (1): 101–22.

Children's Defense Fund. 2020. *The State of America's Children 2020.* www.childrensdefense.org/wp-content/uploads/2020/02/The-State-Of-Americas-Children-2020.pdf.

Cohen, A., & M. Gonchar. 2017. "Cultivating Mindfulness for Educators Using Resources from *The New York Times.*" *The New York Times,* September 7. www.nytimes.com/2017/09/07/learning/lesson-plans/cultivating-mindfulness-for-educators-using-resources-from-the-new-york-times.html.

Cole, S.F., J.G. O'Brien, M.G. Gadd, J. Ristuccia, D.L. Wallace, & J.D. Gregory. 2005. *Helping Traumatized Children Learn: Supportive School Environments for Children Traumatized by Family Violence.* Boston: Massachusetts Advocates For Children.

Craig, S.E. 2016. *Trauma-Sensitive Schools: Learning Communities Transforming Children's Lives, K–5.* New York: Teachers College Press.

Cufaude, J. n.d. "The Art of Facilitative Leadership: Maximizing Others' Contributions." *The Systems Thinker* 15 (10): 2. Accessed December 17, 2019. https://thesystemsthinker.com/the-art-of-facilitative-leadership-maximizing-others-contributions/.

Curry, A. 2019. "Parents' Emotional Trauma May Change Their Children's Biology. Studies in Mice Show How." *Science,* July 18. www.sciencemag.org/news/2019/07/parents-emotional-trauma-may-change-their-children-s-biology-studies-mice-show-how.

Curwin, R.L., A.N. Mendler, & B.D. Mendler. 2008. *Discipline with Dignity: New Challenges, New Solutions*. 3rd ed. Alexandria, VA: ASCD.

Darling-Hammond, L., M.E. Hyler, & M. Gardner. 2017. *Effective Teacher Professional Development*. Palo Alto, CA: Learning Policy Institute, June 5. https://learningpolicyinstitute.org/sites/default/files/product-files/Effective_Teacher_Professional_Development_REPORT.pdf.

de Saint Exupery, A. 1950. *The Wisdom of the Sands*. New York: Harcourt, Brace.

Deci, E., R. Koestner, & R. Ryan. 1999. "A Meta-Analytic Review of Experiments Examining the Effects of Extrinsic Rewards on Intrinsic Motivation." *Psychological Bulletin* 125 (6): 627–68.

Deci, E., R. Koestner, & R. Ryan. 2001. "Extrinsic Rewards and Intrinsic Motivation in Education: Reconsidered Once Again." *Review of Educational Research* 71: 1–27.

Delpit, L. 2006. *Other People's Children: Cultural Conflict in the Classroom*. Updated ed. New York: New Press.

Derman-Sparks, L., & J.O. Edwards with C. Goins. 2020. *Anti-Bias Education for Young Children and Ourselves*. 2nd ed. Washington, DC: NAEYC.

Derman-Sparks, L., D. LeeKeenan, & J. Nimmo. 2015. "Building Anti-Bias Early Childhood Programs: The Role of the Leader." *Young Children* 70 (2): 42–45.

Desautels, L. 2019. "The Role of Emotion Co-Regulation in Discipline." Edutopia, October 15. www.edutopia.org/article/role-emotion-co-regulation-discipline.

Devine, P.G., P.S. Forscher, A.J. Austin, & W.T.L. Cox. 2012. "Long-Term Reduction in Implicit Race Bias: A Prejudice Habit-Breaking Intervention." *Journal of Experimental Social Psychology* 48 (6): 1267–78.

District Leadership Forum. 2019. *Breaking Bad Behavior: The Rise of Classroom Disruptions in Early Grades and How Districts Are Responding*. EAB. http://pages.eab.com/rs/732-GKV-655/images/BreakingBadBehaviorStudy.pdf.

Dodge, K.A., J.D. Coie, G. Pettit, & J. Price. 1990. "Peer Status and Aggression in Boys' Groups: Developmental and Contextual Analyses." *Child Development* 61 (5): 1289–309.

Dreikurs, R. With V. Soltz. 1964. *Children: The Challenge*. New York: Hawthorn.

Driscoll, K.C., & R.C. Pianta. 2010. "Banking Time in Head Start: Early Efficacy of an Intervention Designed to Promote Supportive Teacher-Child Relationships." *Early Education and Development* 21 (1): 38–64.

DuFour, R. 2004. "What Is a Professional Learning Community?" *Educational Leadership* 61 (8): 6–11. www.ascd.org/publications/educational-leadership/may04/vol61/num08/What-Is-a-Professional-Learning-Community¢.aspx.

DuFour, R., & M. Fullan. 2013. *Cultures Built to Last: Systemic PLCs at Work*. Bloomington, IN: Solution Tree Press.

Dunlap, G., P.S. Strain, L. Fox, J.J. Carta, M. Conroy, B.J. Smith, et al. 2006. "Prevention and Intervention with Young Children's Challenging Behavior: Perspectives Regarding Current Knowledge." *Behavioral Disorders* 32 (1): 29–45.

Duran, F.B., K.S. Hepburn, R.K. Kaufmann, L.T. Le, M.D Allen, E.M. Brennan, & B.L. Green. n.d. "Early Childhood Mental Health Consultation: Research Synthesis." The Center on the Social and Emotional Foundations for Early Learning. Accessed June 16, 2019. http://csefel.vanderbilt.edu/documents/rs_ecmhc.pdf.

Durlak, J.A., R.P. Weissberg, A.B. Dymnicki, R.B. Taylor, & K.B. Schellinger. 2011. "The Impact of Enhancing Students' Social and Emotional Learning: A Meta-Analysis of School-Based Universal Interventions." *Child Development* 82 (1): 405–32.

Eberhardt, J.L. 2019. *Biased: Uncovering the Hidden Prejudice That Shapes What We See, Think, and Do*. New York: Viking.

Einhorn, E. 2019. "It Makes Us Better Teachers Because We're Not Carrying It Inside." Chalkbeat Detroit, June 26. https://detroit.chalkbeat.org/2019/6/26/21121089/it-makes-us-better-teachers-because-we-re-not-carrying-it-inside-how-a-detroit-preschool-helps-teach

Eisenberg, N., C. Valiente, T.L. Spinrad, A. Cumberland, J. Liew, M. Reiser, & A. Cumberland. 2009. "Longitudinal Relations of Children's Effortful Control, Impulsivity, and Negative Emotionality to Their Externalizing, Internalizing, and Co-Occurring Behavior Problems." *Developmental Psychology* 45 (4): 988–1008.

Elias, M.J., & Y. Schwab. 2006. "From Compliance to Responsibility: Social and Emotional Learning and Classroom Management." In *Handbook of Classroom Management: Research, Practice, and Contemporary Issues*, eds. C.M. Evertson & C.S. Weinstein, 309–41. Mahwah, NJ: Erlbaum.

Erdman, S., & L.J. Colker. With E.C. Winter. 2020. *Trauma and Young Children: Teaching Strategies to Support and Empower*. Washington, DC: NAEYC.

Espinosa, L.M. 2010. *Getting It Right for Young Children from Diverse Backgrounds: Applying Research to Improve Practice*. Upper Saddle River, NJ: Pearson.

Evans, M.L., M. Lindauer, & M.E. Farrell. 2020. "A Pandemic Within a Pandemic—Intimate Partner Violence During COVID-19." Perspective. *New England Journal of Medicine*, September 16, DOI: 10.1056/NE/Mp2024046. https://www.nejm.org/doi/full/10.1056/NEJMp2024046.

Fabes, R.A., & N. Eisenberg. 1992. "Young Children's Coping with Interpersonal Anger." *Child Development* 63 (1): 116–128.

Feeney, S., & N.K. Freeman. 2018. *Ethics and the Early Childhood Educator: Using The NAEYC Code.* 3rd ed. Washington, DC: NAEYC.

Felitti, V.J., R.F. Anda, D. Nordenberg, D.F. Williamson, A.M. Spitz, V. Edwards, M.K. Koss & J.S. Marks. 1998. "Relationship of Childhood Abuse and Household Dysfunction to Many of the Leading Causes of Death in Adults." *American Journal of Preventive Medicine* 14 (4): 245–58.

Fisher, A.V., K.E. Godwin, & H. Seltman. 2014. "Visual Environment, Attention Allocation, and Learning in Young Children: When Too Much of a Good Thing May Be Bad." *Psychological Science* 25 (7): 1362–370.

Ford, J.E. 2016. "The Root of Discipline Disparities." *Educational Leadership* 74 (3): 42–46.

Forscher P.S., C. Mitamura, E.L. Dix, W.T.L. Cox, & P.G. Devine. 2017. "Breaking the Prejudice Habit: Mechanisms, Timecourse, and Longevity." *Journal of Experimental Social Psychology* 72: 133–46. https://doi.org/10.1016/j.jesp.2017.04.009.

Frick, P.J., & A.S. Morris. 2004. "Temperament and Developmental Pathways to Conduct Problems." *Journal of Clinical Child and Adolescent Psychology* 33 (1): 54–68.

Fullan, M. 2016. *The New Meaning of Educational Change.* 5th ed. New York: Teachers College Press.

Fullan, M., & M. Pinchot. 2018. "The Fast Track to Sustainable Turnaround." *Educational Leadership* 75 (6): 48–54.

GAO (US General Accounting Office). 2018. *K–12 Education: Discipline Disparities for Black Students, Boys, and Students with Disabilities.* GAO-18-258. www.gao.gov/products/gao-18-258.

Gatti, U., & R.E. Tremblay. 2005. "Social Capital and Physical Violence." In *Developmental Origins of Aggression,* eds. R.E. Tremblay, W.W. Hartup, & J. Archer, 398–424. New York: Guilford.

Gay, G. 2010. *Culturally Responsive Teaching: Theory, Research, and Practice.* 2nd ed. New York: Teachers College Press.

Gilliam, W.S. 2005. *Prekindergarteners Left Behind: Expulsion Rates in State Prekindergarten Systems.* FCD Policy Brief Series No. 3. New Haven, CT: Yale University Child Study Center. https://medicine.yale.edu/childstudy/zigler/publications/National%20Prek%20Study_expulsion%20brief_34775_5379_v1.pdf.

Gilliam, W.S. 2007. *Early Childhood Consultation Partnership: Results of a Random-Controlled Evaluation.* New Haven, CT: Yale University Child Study Center.

Gilliam, W.S., & G. Shahar. 2006. "Preschool and Child Care Expulsion and Suspension: Rates and Predictors in One State." *Infants and Young Children* 19 (3): 228–45.

Gilliam, W.S., A.N. Maupin, C.R. Reyes, M. Accavitti, & F. Shic. 2016. "Do Early Educators' Implicit Biases Regarding Sex and Race Relate to Behavior Expectations and Recommendations of Preschool Expulsions and Suspensions?" Yale University Child Study Center. https://medicine.yale.edu/childstudy/zigler/publications/preschool%20implicit%20bias%20policy%20brief_final_9_26_276766_5379_v1.pdf.

Ginsburg, K.R., American Academy of Pediatrics Committee on Communications, & Committee on Psychosocial Aspects of Child and Family Health. 2007. "The Importance of Play in Promoting Healthy Child Development and Maintaining Strong Parent-Child Bonds." *Pediatrics* 119 (1): 182–91.

Goleman, D. 2005. *Emotional Intelligence: Why It Can Matter More Than IQ.* New York: Bantam.

Goleman, D. 2006. *Social Intelligence: The New Science of Human Relationships.* New York: Bantam.

Goleman, D., R. Boyatzis, & A. McKee, A. 2013. *Primal Leadership: Unleashing the Power of Emotional Intelligence.* Boston: Harvard Business Review Press.

Green, B.L., M.C. Everhart, M. Gettman, L. Gordon, & B. Friesen. N.d. *Mental Health Consultation in Head Start: Selected National Findings—Mental Health Services Survey Report.* Accessed August 3, 2019. https://pathwaysrtc.pdx.edu/pdf/pbMHConsultHS.pdf.

Greenberg, M.T., J.L. Brown, & R.M. Abenavoli. 2016. "Teacher Stress and Health: Effects on Teachers, Students, and Schools." Issue brief. Pennsylvania State University, Edna Bennett Pierce Prevention Research Center. www.prevention.psu.edu/uploads/files/rwjf430428.pdf.

Greene, R.W. 2010. *The Explosive Child: A New Approach for Understanding and Parenting Easily Frustrated, Chronically Inflexible Children.* New York: Harper.

Gregory, A., R.J. Skiba, & K. Mediratta. 2017. "Eliminating Disparities in School Discipline: A Framework for Intervention." *Review of Research in Education* 41 (1): 253–78.

Groves, B.A. 2003. *Children Who See Too Much: Lessons from the Child Witness to Violence Project.* Boston: Beacon.

Gunderson, E.A., S.J. Gripshover, C. Romero, C.S. Dweck, S. Goldin-Meadow, & S.C. Levine. 2013. "Parent Praise to 1- To 3-Year-Olds Predicts Children's Motivational Frameworks 5 Years Later." *Child Development* 84 (5): 1526–41.

Guskey, T.R. 2002. "Does It Make A Difference? Evaluating Professional Development." *Educational Leadership* 59 (6): 45–51.

Haimovitz, K., & C. Dweck. 2017. "The Origins of Children's Growth and Fixed Mindsets: New Research and a New Proposal." *Child Development* 88 (6): 1849–59.

Hall, E.T. 1977. *Beyond Culture*. Garden City, NY: Anchor Press/Doubleday.

Hamre, B.K., & R.C. Pianta. 2005. "Can Instructional and Emotional Support in the First-Grade Classroom Make a Difference for Children at Risk of School Failure?" *Child Development* 76 (5): 949–67.

Harris, N.B. 2019. *The Deepest Well: Healing the Long-Term Effects of Childhood Adversity*. Boston: Mariner Books.

Harvard Business School. 2017. *Harvard Business Review Manager's Handbook: The 17 Skills Leaders Need to Stand Out*. Boston: Harvard Business Review Press.

Heath, S.B. 1983. *Ways with Words: Language, Life, and Work in Communities and Classrooms*. New York: Cambridge University Press.

Heathfield. S.M. 2019. "Leadership Vision." The Balance Careers. www.thebalancecareers.com/leadership-vision-1918616.

Hepburn, K.S., D.F. Perry, E.M. Shivers, & W.S. Gilliam. 2013. "Early Childhood Mental Health Consultation as an Evidence-Based Practice: Where Does It Stand?" *ZERO TO THREE* 33 (5): 10–19.

HHS (US Department of Health & Human Services) & ACF (Administration for Children & Families). n.d. "Resource Guide To Trauma-Informed Services." Accessed July 28, 2019. www.acf.hhs.gov/trauma-toolkit/secondary-traumatic-stress.

HHS (US Department of Health & Human Services) & ED (US Department of Education). 2016. "Policy Statement on Expulsion and Suspension Policies in Early Childhood Settings." https://www.acf.hhs.gov/sites/default/files/ecd/expulsion_ps_numbered.pdf.

Howard, T.C. 2019. "Capitalizing on Culture: Engaging Young Learners in Diverse Classrooms." In *Spotlight on Young Children: Equity and Diversity*, eds. C. Gillanders & R. Procopio, 31–44. Washington, DC: NAEYC.

Howell, J., & K. Reinhard. 2015. *Rituals and Traditions: Fostering a Sense of Community in Preschool*. Washington, DC: NAEYC.

Howes, C., C.E. Hamilton, & L.C. Phillipsen. 1998. "Stability and Continuity of Child-Caregiver and Child-Peer Relationships." *Child Development* 69 (2): 418–26.

Institute on Trauma and Trauma-Informed Care. n.d. "What Is Trauma-Informed Care?" University at Buffalo, Buffalo Center for Social Research. Accessed October 26, 2019. http://socialwork.buffalo.edu/social-research/institutes-centers/institute-on-trauma-and-trauma-informed-care/what-is-trauma-informed-care.html.

Jablon, J., A.L. Dombro, & S. Johnsen. 2016. *Coaching with Powerful Interactions: A Guide for Partnering with Early Childhood Teachers*. Washington, DC: NAEYC.

Jennings, P.A. 2018. "Bringing Mindfulness to Teacher PD." *Educational Leadership* 76 (2): 64–68.

Johnson, S.M., S.K. Reinhorn, M. Charner-Laird, M.A. Kraft, M. Ng, & J.P. Papay. 2014. "Ready to Lead, But How? Teachers' Experiences in High-Poverty Urban Schools." *Teachers College Record* 116 (10): 1–50.

Jones, D., & D. Levin. 2016. "Here's Why Preschool Suspensions Are Harmful." *Education Week,* February 23. www.edweek.org/ew/articles/2016/02/24/heres-why-preschool-suspensions-are-harmful.html.

Kabat-Zinn, J. 2003. "Mindfulness-Based Interventions in Context: Past, Present, and Future." *Clinical Psychology: Science and Practice* 10 (2): 144–56.

Kağitçibaşi, Ç. 1996. *Family and Human Development Across Cultures: A View from the Other Side*. Mahwah, NJ: Erlbaum.

Kaiser, B., & J.S. Rasminsky. 2017. *Challenging Behavior in Young Children: Understanding, Preventing, and Responding Effectively*. 4th ed. Columbus, OH: Pearson Education.

Kaiser, B., & J.S. Rasminsky. 1994. "Implementing a Professional Development Policy." *Interaction* (Fall): 13–14.

Kamins, M.L., & C.S. Dweck. 1999. "Person Versus Process Praise and Criticism: Implications for Contingent Self-Worth and Coping." *Developmental Psychology* 35 (3): 835–847.

Karsh, K.G., A.C. Repp, C.M. Dahlquist, & D. Munk. 1995. "In Vivo Functional Assessment and Multi-Element Interventions for Problem Behavior of Students with Disabilities in Classroom Settings." *Journal of Behavioral Education* 5 (2): 189–210.

Katz, L.G. 1972. "The Developmental Stages of Preschool Teachers." *Elementary School Journal* 73 (1): 50–55.

Klass, C.S., K.A. Guskin, & M. Thomas. 1995. "The Early Childhood Program: Promoting Children's Development Through and Within Relationships." *ZERO TO THREE* 16 (2): 9–17.

Kohli, R., & D. Solorzano, D. 2012. "'Teachers, Please Learn Our Names!' Racial Microaggressions and the K–12 Classroom." *Race, Ethnicity and Education* 15 (4): 441–62.

Koralek, D., K. Nemeth, & K. Ramsey. 2019. *Families & Educators Together: Building Great Relationships that Support Young Children*. Washington, DC: NAEYC.

LeeKeenan, D., & I.C. Ponte. 2018. *From Survive to Thrive: A Director's Guide for Leading an Early Childhood Program*. Washington, DC: NAEYC.

Lives in the Balance. n.d. a. "About the CPS Model." Accessed October 8, 2019. www.livesinthebalance.org/about-cps.

Lives in the Balance. n.d. b. "Ending the Cycle of Restraint and Seclusion in Schools." Accessed September 1, 2020. www.livesinthebalance.org/restraint-and-seclusion-in-schools.

Lofthouse, R., D. Leat, & C. Towler. 2010. "Coaching for Teaching and Learning: A Practical Guide for Schools." CFBT Education Trust. https://assets.publishing.service.gov.uk/government/uploads/system/uploads/attachment_data/file/327944/coaching-for-teaching-and-learning.pdf.

Longstreth, S., & S. Garrity. 2018. *Effective Discipline Policies: How to Create a System That Supports Young Children's Social-Emotional Competence.* Lewisville, NC: Gryphon House.

Lynch, E.W. 2011. "Developing Cross-Cultural Competence." In *Developing Cross-Cultural Competence: A Guide for Working with Children and Their Families,* eds. E.W. Lynch & M.J. Hanson, 41–77. 4th ed. Baltimore, MD: Brookes.

Mann, T.C., J. Cone, & M.J. Ferguson. 2015. "Social-Psychological Evidence for the Effective Updating of Implicit Attitudes." *Behavioral and Brain Sciences* 38: E15.

McCabe, L.A., & E.C. Frede. 2007. *Challenging Behaviors and the Role of Preschool Education.* National Institute for Early Education Research Preschool Policy Brief, 16. https://nieer.org/wp-content/uploads/2016/08/16.pdf.

McEwen, B. 2012. The Role of Stress in Physical and Mental Health. In *From Neurons To Neighborhoods: An Update: Workshop Summary,* ed. Institute of Medicine and National Research Council. Washington, DC: National Academies Press.

Meyers, T.W., & T.A. Cornille. 2002. "The Trauma of Working with Traumatized Children." In *Treating Compassion Fatigue,* ed. C.R. Figley, 39–55. New York: Brunner/Routledge.

Michelson, L., & A. Mannarino. 1986. "Social Skills Training with Children: Research and Clinical Applications." In *Children's Social Behavior: Development, Assessment, and Modification,* eds. P.S. Strain, M.J. Guralnick, & H.M. Walker, 373–406. Orlando, FL: Academic Press.

Minahan, J. October 2019. "Trauma-Informed Teaching Strategies." *Educational Leadership* 77 (2): 30–35.

Minahan, J., & N. Rappaport. 2012. *The Behavior Code: A Practical Guide to Understanding and Teaching the Most Challenging Students.* Cambridge, MA: Harvard Education Press.

Mindshift. 2019. "Why Mindfulness and Trauma-Informed Teaching Don't Always Go Together." KQED, January 27. www.kqed.org/mindshift/52881/why-mindfulness-and-trauma-informed-teaching-dont-always-go-together.

Moffitt, T.E., & A. Caspi. 2001. "Childhood Predictors Differentiate Life-Course Persistence and Adolescence-Limited Antisocial Pathways Among Males and Females." *Development and Psychopathology* 13 (2): 355–75.

Murphy, P., & R. George. 2018. "The Why and When of Walkthroughs." *Ed Update* 60 (9): 2–5. www.ascd.org/publications/newsletters/education-update/sept18/vol60/num09/the-why-and-when-of-walkthroughs.aspx.

NAEYC. 2016. "Code of Ethical Conduct and Statement of Commitment". Position statement (brochure). www.naeyc.org/files/naeyc/file/positions/PSETH05.pdf.

NAEYC. 2019. *Advancing Equity in Early Childhood Education.* Position statement. www.naeyc.org/resources/position-statements/equity.

National Child Traumatic Stress Network, Justice Consortium, Schools Committee, and Culture Consortium. 2017. *Addressing Race and Trauma in the Classroom: A Resource for Educators.* Los Angeles, CA, & Durham, NC: National Center for Child Traumatic Stress. www.nctsn.org/sites/default/files/resources/addressing_race_and_trauma_in_the_classroom_educators.pdf.

National Scientific Council on the Developing Child. 2010. *Persistent Fear and Anxiety Can Affect Young Children's Learning and Development.* Working Paper No. 9. https://46y5eh11fhgw3ve3ytpwxt9r-wpengine.netdna-ssl.com/wp-content/uploads/2017/02/How-Persistent-Fear-and-Anxiety-Can-Affect-Young-Childrens-Learning-Behaviour-and-Health.pdf.

National Scientific Council on the Developing Child. 2011. *Building the Brain's "Air Traffic Control" System: How Early Experiences Shape the Development of Executive Functions.* Working Paper No. 11. https://developingchild.harvard.edu/wp-content/uploads/2011/05/How-Early-Experiences-Shape-the-Development-of-Executive-Function.pdf

Nicholson, J., L. Perez, & J. Kurtz. 2019. *Trauma-Informed Practices for Early Childhood Educators: Relationship-Based Approaches That Support Healing and Build Resilience in Young Children.* New York: Routledge.

Office for Civil Rights (Office for Civil Rights, US Department of Education). 2016. "2013–2014. Civil Rights Data Collection: Key Data Highlights on Equity and Opportunity Gaps in Our Nation's Public Schools." www2.ed.gov/about/offices/list/ocr/docs/crdc-2013-14.html.

Okonofua, J.A., D. Paunesku, & G.M. Walton. 2016. "Brief Intervention to Encourage Empathic Discipline Cuts Suspension Rates in Half Among Adolescents." *PNAS* 113 (19): 5221–26.

Olson, S.L., A.J. Sameroff, D.C.R. Kerr, N.L. Lopez, & H.M. Wellman. 2005. "Developmental Foundations of Externalizing Problems in Young Children: The Role of Effortful Control." *Development and Psychopathology* 17 (1): 25–45.

O'Neill, C., & M. Brinkerhoff. 2018. *Five Elements of Collective Leadership for Early Childhood Professionals.* St. Paul, MN, & Washington, DC: Redleaf Press & NAEYC.

O'Neill, R.E., R.W. Albin, K. Storey, R.H. Horner, & J.R. Sprague. 2015. *Functional Assessment and Program Development for Problem Behavior: A Practical Handbook.* 3rd ed. Stamford, CT: Cengage Learning.

Ortiz, R., & E.M. Sibinga. 2017. "The Role of Mindfulness in Reducing the Adverse Effects of Childhood Stress and Trauma." *Children* 4 (3): 16. www.ncbi.nlm.nih.gov/pmc/articles/pmc5368427.

Perry, B. 2014. "The Neurosequential Model of Therapeutics: Application of a Developmentally Sensitive and Neurobiology-Informed Approach to Clinical Problem Solving in Maltreated Children." In *Infant and Early Childhood Mental Health: Core Concepts and Clinical Practice,* eds. K. Brandt, B.D. Perry, S. Seligman, & E. Tronick, 21–54. Arlington, VA: American Psychiatric Publishing.

Platt, R. 2019. "What's Love Got to Do with It?" *Educational Leadership* 77 (2): 42–46.

Porath, S.L. 2018. "A Powerful Influence: An Online Book Club for Educators." *Journal of Digital Learning in Teacher Education* 34 (2): 115–26.

Project Implicit. n.d. *Implicit Association Test.* Accessed May 3, 2019. https://implicit.harvard.edu/implicit/takeatest.html.

Quesenberry, A.C., M.L. Hemmeter, & M.M. Ostrosky. 2011. "Addressing Challenging Behavior in Head Start: A Closer Look at Program Policies and Procedures." *Topics in Early Childhood Special Education* 30 (4): 209–20.

Rattan, A., C. Good, & C.S. Dweck. 2012. "'It's Ok—Not Everyone Can Be Good at Math': Instructors with an Entity Theory Comfort (and Demotivate) Students." *Journal of Experimental Social Psychology* 48 (3): 731–37.

Readdick, C.A., & P.L. Chapman. 2000. "Young Children's Perceptions of Time Out." *Journal of Research in Childhood Education* 15 (1): 81–87.

Redfield, C.A. 2015. "Four Principles for Bias-Busting in the Classroom." *Education Week Teacher,* September 16. www.edweek.org/tm/articles/2015/09/16/four-principles-for-bias-busting-in-the-classroom.html.

Renard, L. 2019. "How to Become a Reflective Teacher—The Complete Guide for Reflection in Teaching." *Bookwidgets Teacher Blog,* February 21. www.bookwidgets.com/blog/2019/02/how-to-become-a-reflective-teacher-the-complete-guide-for-reflection-in-teaching.

Robin, A.L., M. Schneider, & M. Dolnick. 1976. "The Turtle Technique: An Extended Case Study of Self-Control in the Classroom." *Psychology in the Schools* 13 (4): 449–53.

Rossen, E. 2019. "Nine Simple Trauma-Informed Gestures for Educators." *Aces Connection* (blog), March 13. www.acesconnection.com/blog/nine-simple-trauma-informed-gestures-for-educators.

Rothbart, M.K. 2004. "Commentary: Differentiated Measures of Temperament and Multiple Pathways to Childhood Disorders." *Journal of Clinical Child and Adolescent Psychology* 33 (1): 82–87.

Rothbart, M.K., & J.E. Bates. 2006. "Temperament." In *Handbook of Child Psychology: Vol. 3. Social, Emotional, And Personality Development*, series ed. W. Damon & vol. ed. N. Eisenberg, 105–76. 6th ed. New York: Wiley.

Rothbart, M.K., M.I. Posner, & J. Kieras. 2006. "Temperament, Attention, and the Development of Self-Regulation." In *Handbook of Early Childhood Development*, eds. K. McCartney & D. Phillips, 338–57. Malden, MA: Blackwell.

Rothstein-Fisch, C., & E. Trumbull. 2008. *Managing Diverse Classrooms: How to Build on Students' Cultural Strengths.* Alexandria, VA: ASCD.

Rutter, M. 2000. "Resilience Reconsidered: Conceptual Considerations." In *Handbook of Early Childhood Intervention*, eds. J.P. Shonkoff & S.J. Meisels, 651–82. 2nd ed. New York: Cambridge University Press.

Sacks, V., & D. Murphey. 2018. "The Prevalence of Adverse Childhood Experiences, Nationally, by State, and by Race or Ethnicity." Child Trends, February 20. www.childtrends.org/publications/prevalence-adverse-childhood-experiences-nationally-state-race-ethnicity.

Samuels, C.A. 2013. "Tensions Accompany Growth of PBIS Discipline Model." *Education Week,* August 27. www.edweek.org/ew/articles/2013/08/28/2pbis_ep.h33.html.

Schachner, A., K. Belodoff, W.-B. Chen, T. Kutaka, A. Fikes, K. Ensign, et al. 2016. *Preventing Suspensions and Expulsions in Early Childhood Settings: An Administrator's Guide to Supporting All Children's Success.* Menlo Park, CA: SRI International. http://preventexpulsion.org.

Schachter, R.E., & H.K. Gerde. 2019. "Personalized Professional Development: How Teachers Can Use Videos to Improve Their Practice." *Young Children* 74 (4): 55–63.

Schwartz, K. 2019. "Why Mindfulness and Trauma-Informed Teaching Don't Always Go Together." Mindshift, January 28. www.kqed.org/mindshift/52881/why-mindfulness-and-trauma-informed-teaching-dont-always-go-together.

Skiba, R.J., & D.J. Losen. 2015–2016. "From Reaction to Prevention: Turning the Page on School Discipline." *American Educator* 39 (4): 4–11.

Smith, R. 2004. *Conscious Classroom Management: Unlocking the Secrets of Great Teaching.* San Rafael, CA: Conscious Teaching Publications.

Sorrels, B. 2015. *Reaching and Teaching Children Exposed to Trauma.* Lewisville, NC: Gryphon House.

Sparks, S.D. 2019a. "Children May Struggle More With a Noisy Classroom Than Adults." *Education Week* (blog), February 11. http://blogs.edweek.org/edweek/inside-school-research/2019/02/children_may_struggle_more_wit.html.

Sparks, S.D. 2019b. "How Caring for Students in Distress Can Take a Steep Toll." *Education Week* 39 (5): 12–13.

Sperry, R.W. 2011. *Flip It! Transforming Challenging Behavior.* Villanova, PA: Devereux Center for Resilient Children & Lewisville, NC: Kaplan Early Learning Company.

Spiegel, A. 2012. "Teachers' Expectations Can Influence How Students Perform." *Health,* September 17. National Public Radio. www.npr.org/sections/health-shots/2012/09/18/161159263/teachers-expectations-can-influence-how-students-perform.

Statman-Weil, K. 2015. "Creating Trauma-Sensitive Classrooms." *Young Children* 70 (2): 72–79.

Stoll, L., R. Bolam, A. Mcmahon, M. Wallace, & S. Thomas. 2006. "Professional Learning Communities: A Review of the Literature." *Journal of Educational Change* 7: 221–58.

Strayhorn, J.M., & P.S. Strain. 1986. "Social and Language Skills for Preventive Mental Health: What, How, Who, and When." In *Children's Social Behavior: Development, Assessment, and Modification,* eds. P.S. Strain, M.J. Guralnick, & H.M. Walker, 287–330. Orlando, FL: Academic Press.

Sullivan, D.R. 2016. "Spreading the Wealth: Leadership at All Levels." In *Leading Early Childhood Organizations*, 34–37. The Art of Leadership Series. Redmond, WA: Exchange Press.

Sun, K.L. 2015. "There's No Limit: Mathematics Teaching for a Growth Mindset." PhD diss., Stanford University.

Sykes, M. 2014. *Doing the Right Thing for Children: Eight Qualities of Leadership.* St. Paul, MN: Redleaf Press.

Sykes, M. 2016. "The Role of Knowledge in Leadership." In *Leading Early Childhood Organizations*, 30–33. The Art of Leadership Series. Redmond, WA: Exchange Press.

Tang, A., H. Crawford, S. Morales, K.A. Degnan, D.S. Pine, & N.A. Fox. 2020. "Infant Behavioral Inhibition Predicts Personality and Social Outcomes Three Decades Later." *Proceedings of the National Academy of Science* 117 (18): 9800–807. www.pnas.org/content/117/18/9800.

Terada, Y. 2018. "Welcoming Students with a Smile." Edutopia, September 11. www.edutopia.org/article/welcoming-students-smile.

Thapa, A., J. Cohen, S. Guffey, & A. Higgins-D'Alessandro. 2013. "A Review of School Climate Research." *Review of Educational Research* 83 (3): 357–85.

Thomas, A., S. Chess, & H.G. Birch. 1968. *Temperament and Behavior Disorders in Children.* New York: New York University Press.

Tomlinson, C.A. May 2016. "One to Grow On / Caring for Teachers." *Educational Leadership* 73 (8): 92–93.

Tremblay, R.E. 2010. "Developmental Origins of Disruptive Behaviour Problems: The 'Original Sin' Hypothesis, Epigenetics, and Their Consequences for Prevention." *Journal of Child Psychology and Psychiatry* 51 (4): 341–67.

Tremblay, R.E., topic ed. 2012. "Aggression." In *Encyclopedia on Early Childhood Development,* eds. R.E. Tremblay, M. Boivin, & R. Peters. www.child-encyclopedia.com/sites/default/files/dossiers-complets/en/aggression.pdf.

Underwood, M.K. 2003. As *Social Aggression Among Girls.* New York: Guilford Press.

Venet, A.S. 2018. "The How and Why of Trauma-Informed Teaching." Edutopia, August 3. www.edutopia.org/article/how-and-why-trauma-informed-teaching.

Vilen, A. 2017. "What Motivates Teachers to 'Opt In?'" *Education Week* (blog), October 2. http://blogs.edweek.org/edweek/learning_deeply/2017/10/what_motivates_teachers_to_opt_in.html.

Watson, M. With L. Ecken. 2003. *Learning to Trust: Transforming Difficult Elementary Classrooms Through Developmental Discipline.* San Francisco, CA: Jossey-Bass.

Webster-Stratton, C. 1991. *Dina Dinosaur School.* The Teachers and Children Videotape Series. Seattle, WA: The Incredible Years.

Weinstein, C.S., S. Tomlinson-Clarke, & M. Curran. 2004. "Toward a Conception of Culturally Responsive Classroom Management." *Journal of Teacher Education* 55 (1): 25–38.

Williamson, R. 2012. "Coaching Teachers: An Important Principal Role." Research Into Practice. EPI, February. https://files.eric.ed.gov/fulltext/ED538322.pdf.

Wolpow, R., M.M. Johnson, R. Hertel, & S.O. Kincaid. 2009. *The Heart of Learning and Teaching: Compassion, Resiliency, and Academic Success.* Olympia: Washington State Office of Superintendent of Public Instruction (OSPI) Compassionate Schools.

Wright, J. n.d. "Guiding Children by Using Questions." NAEYC. Accessed October 8, 2019. www.naeyc.org/our-work/families/guiding-children-using-questions.

Yogman, M., A. Garner, J. Hutchinson, K. Hirsh-Pasek, & R.M. Golinkoff. 2018. "The Power of Play: A Pediatric Role in Enhancing Development in Young Children." *Pediatrics* 142 (3): 1–17. https://pediatrics.aappublications.org/content/142/3/e20182058.

Youssef, N.A., L. Lockwood, S. Su, G. Hao, & B.P.F. Rutten. 2018. "The Effects of Trauma, with or without PTSD, on the Transgenerational DNA Methylation Alterations in Human Offsprings." *Brain Sciences* 8 (5): 83. doi: 10.3390/brainsci8050083.

Zinsser, K. 2018. "Why Ending Expulsions from U.S. Preschools Requires More Than Passing Laws to Ban Them." Scholars Strategy Network, November 6. https://scholars.org/contribution/why-ending-expulsions-us-preschools-requires-more-passing-laws-ban-them.

Zinsser, K.M., & T.W. Curby. 2014. "Understanding Preschool Teachers' Emotional Support as a Function of Center Climate" SAGE Open, October. https://journals.sagepub.com/doi/pdf/10.1177/2158244014560728.

ABOUT THE AUTHORS

Barbara Kaiser is the coauthor of *Challenging Behavior in Young Children* (now in its 4th edition) and *Meeting the Challenge*. She has taught at Acadia University in Nova Scotia and at Concordia University and College Marie-Victorin in Montreal, Canada, and presented workshops, keynote speeches, and webinars on challenging behavior in the United States, Canada, and throughout the world. Barbara acted as chief consultant for the Mr. Rogers' Family Communications project *Challenging Behaviors: Where Do We Begin?* and for *Facing the Challenge*, an instructional DVD produced by the Devereux Center for Resilient Children. Barbara also developed an intervention to address youth violence; created webinars and guides on bullying for the Nova Scotia Department of Education; and founded and directed two early childhood centers and an after-school program in Montreal. She has given webinars on leadership and on supporting children, families, and staff returning to school and child care programs during the COVID-19 pandemic. Barbara has an MA from McGill University.

Judy Sklar Rasminsky is a freelance writer who specializes in education and health. With coauthor Barbara Kaiser, she has written *Challenging Behavior in Young Children* and *Challenging Behavior in Elementary and Middle School*, which both earned Texty awards from the Text and Academic Authors Association; and *Meeting the Challenge*, a bestseller selected as a comprehensive membership benefit by NAEYC. In addition, the team has authored a guide for Canadian parents, *The Daycare Handbook*, and a fact book for educators on HIV/AIDS. Judy's work has appeared in publications such as the *Reader's Digest* and the *Los Angeles Times*, been anthologized in textbooks, and been honored by the National Institutes of Health. For many years an editor and researcher for book publishers in New York, London, and Montreal, she holds a BA from Stanford University and an MA from Columbia University.

ACKNOWLEDGMENTS

We are extremely grateful for the help of Kathleen Charner, former editor in chief at NAEYC, and Holly Bohart, senior editor, who early on recognized the need for this book. Holly especially has devoted many hours to helping us with the text. Barbara would also like to thank the staff at Narnia, the early childhood center she founded and led for 17 years, who taught her so much about how to support staff, children, and families. And we send a big thank-you to both of our husbands, Martin Hallett and Michael Rasminsky, for their extraordinary patience and support.